In Memory of Millie

TOTAL COVERAGE

Total Coverage

THE COMPLETE INSURANCE

AND SECURITY GUIDE

Darcie Bundy and Stuart Day

PERENNIAL LIBRARY

Harper & Row, Publishers, New York
Cambridge, Philadelphia, San Francisco, Washington
London, Mexico City, São Paulo, Singapore, Sydney

FIRST EDITION

Designer: Sidney Feinberg

Copyeditor: Bruce Emmer

Index by Maro Riofrancos

Library of Congress Cataloging-in-Publication Data

Bundy, Darcie.
    Total coverage.

    Includes index.
    1. Insurance. 2. Security systems. 3. Burglary
protection. 4. Dwellings—Security measures.
5. Self-defense. I. Day, Stuart. II. Title.
HG8051.B846 1987   368′.0029   86-46050
ISBN 0-06-055077-5   87 88 89 90 91 HC 10 9 8 7 6 5 4 3 2 1
ISBN 0-06-096179-1 (pbk.)   87 88 89 90 91 HC 10 9 8 7 6 5 4 3 2 1

Contents

Introduction

Total Coverage is a comprehensive insurance and security sourcebook for all who seek to maximize protection for themselves and their loved ones, their valued personal property and possessions. Its aim is to help you assemble all your vital interests under a *comprehensive protection package,* an umbrella that will leave you and yours exposed to chance as little as possible—from day to day as well as from year to year.

Most of us have a general understanding of what we need protection *against.* We need protection against *illness* and the financial setback that even a minor one can bring (health insurance). We need protection against the *untimely death* of a primary provider and its potentially devastating consequences for family income (life insurance). We need protection as well against prolonged *disability* of a provider—which not only prevents that breadwinner from working but can also bring burdensome medical bills (disability insurance).

Our homes need protection against *fire.* And in a society in which one home in 12 will be broken into this year, we need protection against *burglary* (homeowner's insurance, basic home security, and home security systems). We also need protection from accidents—the motorist who slams into our car (automobile insurance), the door-to-door salesman who trips and falls over a toy on our front steps and sues (personal liability insurance). And sad as it is, we are all aware that children, women, and the elderly have particular protection needs against people who would harm them (personal safety).

But in spite of our general understanding of what we need protection against, how often does that translate into specifics, into a comprehensive insurance and security action plan? Often as not, the "Achilles heel" is our own optimistic assumption that "it can't happen to us," that we've "already got it covered." That's where so many of us get it wrong—right from the start.

To illustrate, let us pose a few basic questions. Our research indicates that most of us either won't have the answers to these questions or will get the answers wrong.

Start with insurance. Americans spend an average 11 percent of their disposable income on insurance—but, unfortunately, that doesn't add up to "having it all covered." Most of us are uninsured or underinsured in some key areas and wastefully overinsured in others. For example, is your home insured for a minimum of 80 percent of its replacement (not market) value? If you bought it some time ago and haven't upped your homeowner's insurance since, chances are you're dangerously underinsured. If you don't have coverage to 80 percent of replacement value, your insurer will penalize you badly in the event of a partial loss.

If you're like most homeowners covered by a standard policy, you assume it covers for damage to your home caused by flood. Wrong! That requires separately purchased flood insurance. And few of us realize the inadequacy of a standard homeowner's policy, which covers personal belongings for only 50 percent of the coverage on the house itself. That's usually far less than what your personal belongings could be replaced for in the event of a major fire. And do you have a special replacement-cost contents provision in your policy? You should. If not, all you'd get would be purchase price minus depreciation—just pennies on the dollar.

Americans spend more than $111 billion annually on health insurance, but few really understand the coverage they do or don't have. Do you know how "deductibles," "co-insurance," "reasonable and customary fee limits," "exclusions," and "stop losses" determine your out-of-pocket expenses? Do you understand the new federal law that gives you valuable group health conversion rights if your employer lays you off? Does your group plan offer any financial incentives you should be taking advantage of, such as higher reimbursement for generic drugs or outpatient surgery? Are mail-order health policies a good deal or a rip-off? How do you identify a good Medicare supplement policy?

What about the new alternative health care plans today? Do you know anything about the alphabet soup of HMOs, PPOs, and MMSs? They deserve investigation, as they have the potential of saving you an average 25 percent on your medical bills. What are the drawbacks of these new plans?

Life insurance is certainly a subject in need of disentangling. Who needs life insurance? How much? What kind? Did you know that policy prices can vary by 100 percent or more for the same coverage, yet only one in five of us comparison-shops for a policy? What about experimenting with the latest twist, like "universal life" with its month-by-month premium? Who does it protect more, you or the insurance company? Are you interested in a list of the lowest-cost life insurance companies?

Are you among the majority of Americans without adequate disability income insurance? What is "adequate"? Is mortgage insurance a good substitute? And what about automobile insurance? Is your car's value sufficiently greater than the annual comprehensive and collision premiums you're paying to justify the level of coverage? Are you carrying too little liability coverage? Do you understand no-fault insurance? How do you qualify for car insurance discounts?

You don't need an insurance analyst to decipher these and other thorny questions. As a layperson, what you need is to disentangle the subject right from the start by separating key concepts and facts from the undergrowth of trade jargon and "expert" explanations that usually drive newcomers to buy the first insurance package anyone offers them.

Now consider security. Physical security for you and security for your home and your possessions constitute the second aspect of *Total Coverage.* Like insurance, domestic safety and security require careful planning. But even more than insurance—which is, to a large degree, protection on paper —physical security is very much a "hands-on" proposition.

According to a recent poll, 40 percent of Americans feel unsafe even in the privacy of their own homes. As the crime rate soars, everyone is vulnerable. A recent Department of Justice survey confirms our fears, showing that one-third of all assaults and three-fifths of all rapes occur during burglaries. Yet studies show that delaying a burglar as little as four minutes is generally enough to prevent forced entry into your home or apartment. Do you know the relatively simple techniques for causing that critical delay? What kind of landscaping and external lighting should you have, and where? What kind of locks? What are the pros and cons of a guard dog? Do you need an electronic security system? What kind? What features should you look for? And what will it cost? Should you keep a firearm? What personal safety techniques should you teach a child? Would you know what to do for a choking or heart attack victim?

Finally, no one is totally covered without a valid will. Yet as many as seven in ten Americans die without writing a will, thus vastly complicating the inheritance process and often depriving beneficiaries of what otherwise would have been theirs. Dying "intestate" costs your heirs unnecessary time and money.

As you can see, *Total Coverage* is a book for you, the individual consumer. It does not cover commercial or business insurance, professional malpractice insurance, and so on. Moreover, *Total Coverage* focuses on the big items. It doesn't get bogged down in chronicling every kind of specialty insurance and security (generally bad consumer buys anyway) but instead concentrates on what you truly need to protect yourselves and your property.

Does all this sound intimidating, maybe even overwhelming? It really doesn't have to be, if you're willing to spend a little time with it. *Total Coverage* will help. We suggest that you begin by reading the book through fairly quickly. In terms of priorities, it's all in the right order. Insure your health, then your life and income. Follow basic personal and family safety procedures. Insure your home and protect it from fire, natural perils, and theft. Insure your car, with liability being the main concern. And to close the circle of protection, prepare a will. Reading the book through will give you an overview and a sense of where the critical gaps are in your protection. Then you can focus more directly on the chapters you need most. These chapters will give you the basic definitions, terms, principles, and guidelines to use to analyze your own specific needs. They point out pitfalls and "pitches" to avoid. They give specific recommendations of reputable companies, policies, and products for your consideration. They'll tell you what to expect to pay and how to get the most for your money. And each chapter contains a short summary to help keep you focused on the basics, to remind you of the key points and priorities, and to help cut down your rereading time.

By the time you complete your initial reading of *Total Coverage,* you will have recognized that insurance is a form of security and that security is another form of insurance. Because it all boils down to protection—to taking a practical, aggressive, cost-effective approach to consolidating your insurance and security needs into a tight network and to upgrading your protection-mindedness to the same levels as the demands placed on it by today's world. Against the backdrop of some rather weighty subject matter—life, death, health, personal safety, home security—*Total Coverage* takes the brighter view that you *can* take control to a vital degree. With a little effort, you can become as much of an expert as you need to be. By knowing what to do and doing it, you can protect and safeguard all that you care most about.

I

Personal Protection

- **INSURANCE**

- **SECURITY**

Total Coverage is intended to provide guidelines to the reader about insurance and security, not complete information. As each situation is unique, the reader should consult with a competent professional on questions specific to the reader to ensure that the situation has been evaluated carefully and the choice of coverage is appropriate.

The names used in the examples in this book have been changed.

1

Health Insurance

HEALTH CARE COSTS FOR THE NATION APPROACHED $470 BILLION IN 1986 AND ARE EXPECTED TO INCREASE 10 PERCENT BETWEEN 1987 AND 1988.

ALTHOUGH THE MAJORITY OF AMERICANS HAVE SOME FORM OF HEALTH INSURANCE, MANY HAVE ONLY LIMITED COVERAGE, AND SOME 37 MILLION HAVE NO HEALTH INSURANCE AT ALL.

Comprehensive health insurance is a vital component of total coverage. Today the health insurance industry is changing rapidly, presenting consumers with a bewildering array of new choices that make informed decision making all the tougher. Yet being informed goes a long way to determining how protected you are. So let's unravel the health insurance puzzle.

Who's Covered?

Nearly 170 million Americans have some kind of health insurance. Most of us are covered by group plans at work, as health insurance is the most common employee benefit provided by employers. There are, however, big differences in the quality of the plans offered. You have a better chance of having comprehensive health insurance coverage if you work for a *large* company or organization, if you work in the industrialized Northeast or any major urban area, or if you are a member of a strong union that negotiates health insurance contracts with your employer.

But about 36 million Americans have individually purchased plans, either because they're self-employed or work for small organizations not offering health insurance benefits. Individually purchased plans and small group plans (less than 25 people) are usually more expensive—by 15 to 50 percent —than large group plans and are less comprehensive.

Finally, in 1986, roughly 37 million Americans had no health insurance at all—up from 33 million in 1982. This includes at least 4.5 million women between the ages of 40 and 65 and 8 million children. It also includes large numbers of young adults, who are almost twice as likely as any other age group to be without this vital protection. People with annual incomes of $10,000 or less are also often uninsured (although many qualify for some form of public medical assistance). So even though the overall extent of health insurance coverage in this country is encouraging, there are some major gaps. In addition, many of us who have insurance in fact have only *limited coverage*.

Let's analyze what goes into making a good health insurance package. If you have a policy, you can see if it measures up; if you don't have a policy, you can see what you need to look for when purchasing one.

What Is a Comprehensive Health Insurance Package?

Your goal should be to have *comprehensive health insurance* coverage. This doesn't mean you won't have out-of-pocket medical expenses. Even with comprehensive health insurance, you'll still have these expenses (and we'll tell you how to estimate them a little later). But a comprehensive health insurance plan does mean that you and your family are protected from financial ruin by a major illness or accident, and it does mean that a substantial portion of even your more routine medical expenses will be reimbursed. A comprehensive plan is made up of *Basic Protection* and *Major Medical*. If you don't have both, whether your insurance is through a group or is individually purchased, you don't have comprehensive coverage.

Basic protection consists of two parts: *hospitalization* and *physician*

4

expense services. Hospitalization benefits are the most widely held form of health insurance. Generally they cover all or a high percentage (generally 80 percent) of the costs of the hospital room (at the semiprivate rate; if you insist on privacy, you'll pay the difference), board, general nursing care, in-hospital medications, lab work, X rays, intravenous fluids, use of anesthesia equipment, nursery incubator, and so on.

Many hospitalization policies also include *surgical expense benefits*— you're covered for the hospital stay plus the surgeon's bill for the operation or procedure that put you there. More than 165 million Americans have surgical expense benefits as part of their hospitalization package. The most complete hospitalization coverage also includes private-duty nursing. Hospitalization policies are offered by many commercial companies, but 60 percent of insured Americans have coverage through nonprofit Blue Cross plans. All Blue Cross plans work by setting contracts with "participating" hospitals and in effect result in almost all your hospital costs' being covered. Don't, however, assume that all Blue Cross plans are alike. They're not! Each plan is the result of a specific negotiation between the buyer and the local Blue Cross. So inform yourself about the specific benefits provided under your plan, especially noting how many days of hospitalization are covered.

Physician expense benefits are less commonly held than hospitalization insurance. They are not to be confused with the surgical expense benefits that are usually part of a hospitalization policy, as just discussed. Physician expense benefits cover doctor visits while you're in the hospital, assistant surgeon fees, and usually some kinds of office and home doctors' visits, generally when you're ill or being treated for a certain disorder. They do not cover routine physical checkups (which can cost up to $350; many of us don't have them because we have to pay for them out of our own pockets) or related exams or laboratory work—for example, routine gynecological checkups, Pap tests, well-baby visits, and immunizations.

Physician expense benefits are offered by the nonprofit Blue Shield organization as well as by commercial companies. While many people have Blue Cross hospitalization and Blue Shield physician expense benefits, it's also common to carry both parts of your basic protection from a commercial company like Travelers.

Hospitalization plus physician expense benefits make up basic coverage. Where basic coverage leaves off, *major medical* steps in. It covers hospital and medical services beyond the level of basic benefits—that is, when those benefits run out. Major medical provides protection against catastrophic ex-

5

penses of prolonged illness and hospitalization; given the cost of hospitals and doctor care today, "prolonged" can mean as short as a few weeks! Maximum benefits under major medical are generally very high. More than 80 percent of us with this coverage have benefits of $1 million or more, and a full third have unlimited benefits.

Because major medical is not intended to pay for routine or ordinary expenses, its deductible is generally very high, up to $5000. But this isn't as bad as it sounds because that deductible will usually be satisfied by payments made under your basic protection coverage. Fortunately, major medical has become widely available in recent years, so the majority of us are protected to an important degree from the financial disaster a prolonged illness would otherwise bring.

To summarize, a comprehensive health insurance package consists of a hospitalization policy plus physician expense benefits (basic protection) plus major medical. If you have a policy, be sure to check that it offers both of these components.

How to Estimate Your Out-of-Pocket Expenses

Even if you're lucky enough to have comprehensive health insurance, you will have out-of-pocket medical expenses associated with a surgical operation, an illness, or an accident. And these expenses may even be substantial. The only likely exception is if husband and wife each have separate comprehensive policies through their respective workplaces. In that situation, if the woman, say, needs an appendectomy, she would receive all the benefits due her through her own policy, leaving the unreimbursed balance available for coverage under her husband's policy. This is called *coordination of benefits*, and it sometimes results in 100 percent reimbursement of medical expenses. Careful coordination of benefits on the part of insurers is practiced today so that you don't collect twice for medical expenses if you have coverage under two separate policies. People used to get away with that—they made money off their medical treatment. Nowadays insurers work hard to see that benefits are not duplicated.

In any case, most of us don't have such double coverage and, as a result, do have unreimbursed medical expenses. What follows will help you understand the extent of coverage under your policy and how to calculate and anticipate the expenses that your insurance will not reimburse.

The first expense is often the insurance premium itself. Health insurance premiums are obviously affected by the cost of medical care, and both are increasing at faster rates than inflation. In 1986, comprehensive family health insurance policies generally cost $2000 to $3000 a year, depending in part on the region of the country. (If your plan costs much less, chances are you don't have comprehensive coverage.) Individually purchased plans can be 15 to 50 percent more expensive than group coverage.

Obviously, if you have an individual plan, you're personally responsible for all premiums. If, however, you're covered by a group plan through work, find out if it's contributory or noncontributory. *Noncontributory* means your employer pays 100 percent of the premiums—lucky you. *Contributory* means that you and your employer share the payment of premiums. Given rising costs, employers have increasingly opted for contributory plans requiring employees to bear anywhere from 10 to 50 percent of the premium. (It's important to note that many employers do pay 100 percent for a single employee plus one dependent, usually a spouse, but require an employee contribution for family coverage, such as the inclusion of a child.) In recent years, premiums have risen significantly with inflation, so that an employee's dollar contribution to the plan has often increased significantly, even if the employer hasn't changed the percentage share for which the employee is responsible.

Next you want to know how your plan pays benefits. A policy with *inside benefits* will pay only a fixed amount for your hospital room, regardless of the actual rate, or cover your surgical or other doctor's expenses at only a fixed limit, no matter what the actual charges. Payment is usually in cash to you. If your policy pays inside benefits, keep tabs on the going rates for hospital rooms and surgical expenses in your area, and buy supplemental coverage when the rates get appreciably higher than the inside limits of your present policy.

A far better arrangement is a policy offering *service benefits,* sometimes called a "percentage benefit schedule." This is an entitlement to receive specified hospital and surgical care rather than cash. Service benefits have long been the trend in hospitalization insurance and frequently result in "full-payment" coverage for a semiprivate room, board, and in-hospital services, paid directly to the hospital. About 90 percent of people covered by employee group plans have this superior service benefits arrangement. (Many individual plans, in contrast, pay inside limits, as do many mail-order plans, which will be discussed shortly.)

The *deductible* is the dollar amount of medical expenses you must pay out of your own pocket each year before the insurance policy starts paying. Usually the deductible applies to major medical and to physician expense benefits, but increasingly it is applied to hospitalization, too. Deductibles under group plans are commonly in the $150 to $250 range. These deductibles are applied per person covered by the plan—that is, you pay the first, say, $200 of medical expenses for each member of the family before insurance takes over. However, better plans offer an annual maximum family deductible, which allows a family to pool expenses to reach a maximum deductible that's set lower than would result from the per-person rate. Also, a deductible carryforward feature is desirable, whereby bills incurred in the last three months of a calendar year that go toward satisfaction of the deductible can be carried forward to count for the next year's deductible. This too can be a real money saver, although many employers are eliminating carryforwards in a cost-reduction effort today.

The next factor that directly affects your out-of-pocket expenses is *co-insurance,* the arrangement whereby you and the insurer share the cost of your medical treatment. Full-service hospitalization benefits are frequently not subject to co-insurance, but physician expense benefits and major medical are. Typically, the insurer pays 80 percent of these costs, *after* you've satisfied the deductible, and you pay 20 percent. The ratio of some policies is 75 to 25. This co-insurance factor can result in significant out-of-pocket expense.

Sandra S., for example, visits her allergist monthly, with charges of $50 a visit, and she is covered by a plan with a $150 deductible and 80 percent co-insurance. Over the course of a year she will be reimbursed only $360 of her total $600 bill, calculated as follows:

$$\$600 - \$150 \text{ (deductible)} = \$450 \times 80\% \text{ (co-insurance)} = \$360$$

Yet another feature that can result in major out-of-pocket expense is the *reasonable and customary fee limitation.* This is a charge for health care that, according to the insurer, is consistent with the "going rate" for identical or similar services within a specific geographic area. Typically (after satisfaction of the deductible), a policy will pay 80 percent (co-insurance) of expenses up to the "reasonable and customary" fee and no more. Physician expense benefits are the main service affected. If your doctor charges fees in excess of what the insurer deems "reasonable and customary," you pay the difference. Watch out for this limitation! It can leave you with big unreimbursed doctor's bills, especially in urban areas where physicians often charge a wide

8

range of fees for the same service. If, for example, your doctor charges $1500 for hernia repair and your insurer says $1100 is "reasonable and customary," here's how to figure your out-of-pocket expense for the operation:

$$\begin{array}{rl}
\$1100 & \text{reasonable and customary fee} \\
       & \text{for the procedure} \\
- \ 200 & \text{average deductible} \\
\hline
\$ \ 900 & \\
\times \ \ 80\% & \text{co-insurance} \\
\hline
\$ \ 720 & \text{paid by insurer}
\end{array}$$

$$\begin{array}{rl}
\$1500 & \text{surgeon's fee} \\
- \ 720 & \text{paid by insurer} \\
\hline
\$ \ 780 & \text{paid by you}
\end{array}$$

A few years ago, a woman friend had a problem because of "reasonable and customary" fee limits. She found out after the fact that her obstetrician's fee for a major surgical procedure was 100 percent above what her insurer said was "reasonable and customary"—$3000 versus $1500! After her $200 deductible and 80 percent co-insurance, the insurer offered to pay only $1040 of the total bill, leaving $1960 to be paid by the patient. The story has a happy ending, however. With the help of her employee relations department at work, she exercised her right to protest under the policy (which was a major group plan), taking the protest all the way to the insurer's national headquarters. After six months of wrangling, the insurer finally agreed to use the $3000 figure to calculate benefits, and the woman's out-of-pocket expenses dropped to $400.

To avoid a situation such as this, ask your doctor up front about the fee for the procedure in question, then call your insurer and ask what the "reasonable and customary" limit is for that procedure. If your doctor's charge is substantially higher, say so—perhaps you can negotiate the charge down. Sometimes a doctor will agree to take what the insurer will pay as payment in full. If your doctor won't budge, you may want to use the information obtained to comparison-shop for another physician.

Exclusions can result in significant uncovered medical expenses. These are specific conditions (often spelled out in *riders* to the policy), circumstances, or treatments listed in a policy for which the insurer will not pay benefits. Usually, a preexisting condition—a health problem you had before becoming insured—is excluded from coverage, at least for a stipulated period. Frequently, there's an 11-month to two year waiting period for coverage of a preexisting condition. Note that some policies specifically stipulate that they won't cover a pregnancy if conceived within a certain number of months following enrollment in the plan.

Don't try to "cheat" on your health insurance application about a preexisting condition. If you're found out, you'll invalidate all your coverage, not just that for the preexisting condition. Policies define preexisting conditions differently, so if you have such a condition, read the relevant section of your policy very carefully.

Here are some other common exclusions to health insurance policies:

- Procedures that are not medically necessary (e.g., cosmetic surgery)
- Treatment of self-inflicted injuries
- Health care while in active military service, treatment given in a government (e.g., veterans') hospital, and injuries resulting from warfare
- Personal comfort items (such as TV rental) for your hospital room
- Private hospital room
- Treatment payable under workers' compensation
- Custodial care, as in a nursing home
- So-called experimental procedures (e.g., *in vitro* fertilization)
- Eyeglasses and hearing aids

Next, check the *waiting period* designated by the policy. This tells you when coverage actually begins—a certain number of days after you've signed the policy. Obviously, you'd like as short a period as possible. Shoot for 30 days.

Some older policies differentiate coverage for *illness versus accident,* paying for the latter but limiting protection on the former. If you have a policy that's been in force for a while, make sure this undesirable feature is not a part of it. You need financial protection from a prolonged bout of pneumonia just as much as you do for injuries sustained in a car crash.

Finally, better health insurance plans offer a feature that can help limit your out-of-pocket expenses. Called an *out-of-pocket maximum* or *stop loss,* this is the maximum dollar amount of out-of-pocket expenses you must pay in a calendar year before your policy steps in to pick up 100 percent of covered charges at the reasonable and customary level. (Charges that the insurer says are in excess of reasonable and customary fees are excluded from this out-of-pocket limit.) Obviously, the lower the stop loss, the better for you. Usual stop losses range from $1000 to $5000 per family under group plans, but these are increasing as employers try to shift a bigger portion of their skyrocketing medical bills to the consumers of those services. Stop losses are available to both group and individual policyholders.

These are the key terms and concepts that establish what is and isn't covered under a health insurance policy. If you know your policy's deductible, co-insurance factor, exclusions and limitations, and way of paying benefits, you can accurately calculate what your out-of-pocket expenses are likely to be for any particular procedure once you've established the insurer's reasonable and customary fee limit.

Let's summarize, then, the features that make up a good, comprehensive health insurance package. If you already have a policy (whether a group plan through work or an individually purchased plan), see how it stacks up. If you don't yet have coverage, these are the things you should be looking for in a purchase (more specifics on shopping for health insurance appear at the end of the chapter).

- Basic protection plus major medical. Basic protection includes *hospitalization, physician expense benefits,* and, under the best plans, *surgical expense benefits.* Major medical covers hospital and medical expenses when basic protection runs out.
- Under major medical, maximum benefits of at least $250,000 (preferably $1 million) for each person covered under the plan and reinstated annually.
- A plan that pays *service benefits*—an entitlement for specified hospital and surgical benefits—rather than *inside benefits,* a set dollar amount of cash per day of hospitalization.
- A good major group policy will have a deductible of $250 per person or less. With an individual policy, it's better to take a deductible in the $500 range to keep your premium down. (More on this later.) Good policies also offer advantageous *maximum family deductibles* and *deductible carryforwards.*
- A plan that will require you to *co-insure* or pay for no more than 20 percent of your qualified medical care.
- A plan with clearly defined procedures of complaint so that you know how to go about protesting a settlement you think is unfair.

11

- A plan that clearly lists its exclusions and inclusions—that is, what it does and doesn't cover.
- A plan that pays for medical treatment resulting from both *accident* and *illness.*
- A waiting period of no more than 30 days.
- A *stop loss* of no more than $2500 per family for a group plan or $5000 per family under an individual plan.

What the Latest "Twists" in Health Insurance Mean to You

There are many new "twists" in health insurance today. If you're aware of them in advance, you can frequently turn them to your advantage. If you're not, they can end up costing you more in out-of-pocket expense. Let's see what these are.

To set the stage, you need to understand that, on average, employers today pay a whopping 11 percent of their overall payroll for health insurance benefits—more than $100 billion in 1985. That's up $40 billion from 1980 alone. In 1985, employers' average medical care cost per employee was $1770, up 300 percent since 1976. It's no surprise, then, that employers have scrambled to find ways to slow the increase in these expenditures.

What employers tried first was to shift costs to employees. We have described some of this effort already. More plans became *contributory*—for the first time, the employee was required to share the cost of the premium. Plans that were already contributory increased the share of the premium the employee paid. Co-insurance factors for employees were increased. In addition, since 1983, more than 50 percent of companies increased the deductible under their employee group plans.

Since 1985, however, employers have focused on a new strategy for health care cost containment. It can be characterized as an "interventionist" strategy, whereby insurers and employers are no longer merely standing at the sidelines and waiting for the bills to come in. They are intervening in the health care delivery system by actually helping to make decisions about patient care in order to control costs. Chances are you've already been affected by this new strategy. It boils down to three efforts:

- Encouraging employees, with financial incentives, to use health care more cost-effectively
- Reviewing costs and auditing health care payments

- Encouraging and promoting competition among health care providers to help control long-term costs

Here are some specific examples of this strategy of health care cost containment:

- *Second opinions.* Today roughly two-thirds of employer health insurance plans require second opinions for certain major surgical procedures, and roughly 15 percent require them for all procedures. Nearly all employers provide 100 percent coverage for these second opinions.
- *Ambulatory surgery.* Nearly 50 percent of employers will reimburse you with no deductible and at a higher rate (generally 90 percent) if you have minor surgery done on an outpatient basis— that is, without a formal, overnight hospital check-in. Note that a procedure can be considered as outpatient even if actually done in a hospital, so long as you don't stay overnight. For many operations, you can arrive at the hospital in the early morning and leave by midafternoon to qualify as ambulatory or outpatient procedures. Outpatient surgery is also routinely performed at many of the new freestanding medical clinics springing up in shopping centers. Costs at these centers can be 75 percent less than at a hospital just a few blocks away.
- *Precertification.* A method of confirming, by way of second opinion, that hospital admission is, first, medically necessary and, second, of the least necessary duration.
- *Preadmission and outpatient testing.* An increasing number of plans provide higher reimbursement for tests conducted prior to a hospital admission because preadmission testing can result in shorter hospital stays. Outpatient tests are often reimbursed at a 90 percent rate rather than at the standard 80 percent co-insurance rate.
- *Hospital continued-stay review.* This follows precertification and aims to ensure that an appropriately certified admission is not later encumbered by major expenses not part of the admissions review.
- *Employee hospital bill review.* One major study found that 80 to 90 percent of hospital bills contain errors. To encourage employee review of hospital bills, one study showed that more than 25 per-

cent of companies give employees a percentage of any hospital overcharges they discovered.

- *Generic drug use.* Some policies will reimburse you at 90 to 100 percent for generic drugs, because these cost less than brand-name drugs. Brand-name products are reimbursed at a lesser rate, usually 80 percent.
- *Home health care.* The vast majority of insurers and employers now reimburse for many kinds of home health care—nursing and rehabilitation, for example—that can substantially reduce hospital stays.
- *Hospice care.* Reimbursement for hospice care, whether at home or facility-based, is also up substantially.
- *Case management and utilization review.* These are two "catch-all" phrases that cover other items on this list. The main purpose of a case management or utilization program is to ensure that the care in question is necessary; that it is conducted in the least expensive, most appropriate facility; that the treatment plan is reasonable and cost-effective; and that any postdischarge services, such as home health care, are coordinated. Altogether, about 30 percent of U.S. businesses providing medical benefits to employees now use a review service. If you, the patient, or the doctor fails to call in the review board, insurance coverage can be reduced or even eliminated. To be doubly sure you use the reviews, many employers and insurers will lower your co-insurance share and/or waive deductibles. Supporters of utilization review maintain that even with such increased benefits to the employee, the review system cuts medical bills anywhere from 13 to 22 percent.

The final step that employers and insurers are taking is outright intervention in the traditional fee-for-service health care delivery system in an effort to create new competitive forces in the health care industry. Insurers are promoting the development of alternative delivery systems, such as health maintenance organizations (HMOs), preferred provider organization (PPOs), and managed medical systems (MMSs)—new options that are discussed in Chapter 2.

To give you an example of what these new health insurance twists can mean to you, let us tell you about Sydney L., a friend from New Orleans whose health insurance is provided by her employer. Sydney needed a laparoscopy, which is a procedure calling for a small incision in the navel and the insertion of a tiny fiber-optic tube that allows the doctor to see the fallopian tubes and ovaries. Without asking any questions, Sydney checked into the hospital on a Thursday afternoon, had a battery of presurgical tests, and was operated on Friday morning.

Although Sydney was wide awake and feeling fine by 2 o'clock Friday afternoon, her doctor didn't return to the hospital to see her and to sign checkout papers until Saturday afternoon. The hospital counted it as a three-day stay, and the bill for tests, room and board, and operating and recovery rooms was just under $1700. The obstetrician's bill for the procedure was $1200. So Sydney submitted $2900 in expenses to her health insurer, assuming that the insurer would cover it.

Not quite. First, the insurer maintained that the doctor's fee exceeded the reasonable and customary limit by $400. So the insurer calculated Sydney's reimbursement from the $800 limit, minus a $200 deductible, at the 80 percent co-insurance rate—a total of $480 on a $1200 doctor's bill! Then, since her employer had recently added a $250 deductible to its hospitalization policy, Sydney had to pay that amount herself right off the top on the hospital bill. She also had to pay 20 percent of the charges on her presurgical tests. These came to another $120. The insurer also maintained that Sydney and her doctor should have requested an advance utilization review prior to this nonemergency surgery. They insisted that she had stayed in the hospital unnecessarily long and, in fact, that the procedure could have been performed on an outpatient basis. So in essence, the insurer was contesting practically the whole hospital bill. Finally, after two months of haggling, Sydney got her Human Resources people involved. They interceded for her with the insurer and asked for an exception on the basis that the utilization review program was a new part of the company's health insurance plan and that it had not been adequately "advertised" and explained to employees. The insurer agreed to settle the balance of the hospital bill on that basis. Still, Sydney was out $1090, in large part because she didn't understand how to "work" her health insurance. (Incidentally, don't get the idea that only influential Human Resources groups can mediate settlements such as this with insurers. They're nice to have on your side, but Sydney could probably have accomplished the same thing without their help.)

Sydney could have saved herself several hundred dollars by asking her insurer about the reasonable and customary fee limit for the operation. To handle it correctly, she should have discussed the higher-than-average fee with the doctor, who might have lowered his charge, or she might have shopped for another doctor or at least made advance preparations for having to make up the cost difference out of her own pocket. Next, Sydney should have asked if the procedure could be done on an outpatient basis. Laparoscopies are, in fact, commonly handled that way, with presurgical testing also done on an outpatient basis. Not only would she have avoided an unnecessary three-day hospital stay, but she would also have qualified for insurance reimbursement for both the doctor's fee and the presurgical tests at the 90 percent rate. To save all this money, all Sydney needed to do was understand both the basics and the new twists of her health insurance policy.

While most doctors and hospitals, and even many patients, don't like this new interventionist strategy on the part of insurers and employers, you can see from Sydney's story that these techniques will lower not just your insurer's medical expenses but yours too, both in the immediate form of less out-of-pocket expenses and the long-term form of more stable premiums. So be sure you recognize and take advantage of any financial incentives offered by your policy for preadmission testing, generic drug use, hospital bill audits, ambulatory services, and home-based health care. Looked at the opposite way, you should understand how you can be financially penalized, with lower or even eliminated benefits, if you don't follow these new twists in the health insurance game.

Cafeteria Benefit Plans

About 25 percent of employers with benefit plans today offer "cafeteria" plans. You hear a lot about these plans, under which health insurance benefits are linked with other benefits such as vacation time, extra life insurance, and dependent care coverage. With cafeteria plans, employees are generally given a set of basic benefits and then the chance to choose among various special-benefit options. For example, you might be offered more vacation time for less comprehensive health coverage or simply a very high health insurance deductible. Or you might decide to forgo dental insurance altogether and take a subsidy for child care.

Sometimes an employer will set up a *flexible reimbursement* or *spending account,* against which an employee can draw to pay for expanded health or life insurance, financial counseling, legal fees, or dependent care costs. An employee "mixes and matches" according to personal preferences.

Our advice on this is to be very conservative about trading off any of your health insurance for other benefits unless the family is lucky enough to have

16

a duplicate comprehensive policy through the other working spouse. It might be tempting for a healthy young man or woman to opt for an extra two weeks' vacation at the expense of a substantially higher co-insurance factor. But what if that employee is suddenly subject to major surgery and prolonged subsequent medical treatment? The extra vacation quickly pales in comparison to the potential unreimbursed medical expenses.

Some companies have also set up specific medical "expense accounts" for their employees, against which they can draw to pay medical expenses throughout the year. As an incentive to file fewer and lower claims, the company gives the employee all or some of the money left over in the account at the end of the year (or sometimes at retirement). We advise that you also be wary of this cash incentive system. First of all, some companies use it just as a "sweetener" to make higher deductibles or co-insurance more palatable. In the end, you really don't benefit much—in fact, you're worse off if you have a serious illness. Moreover, there is a possible risk in paying an employee *not* to go to the doctor. Neglecting minor ailments in order to get the cash from the account at year's end may allow those ailments to turn into more serious health problems. These cash incentive plans also discourage preventive health care, which can have the same negative effect and can also result in higher long-term medical costs for everyone.

Other Kinds of Health Insurance

Indemnity policies. An indemnity policy is a kind of health insurance that pays you direct cash benefits when you're incurring health care costs. It does not pay for your hospital or doctor bills, although it's usually linked to hospitalization—that is, it pays you cash when you're hospitalized. Indemnity policies are generally advertised and sold through the mail or on television. They offer to pay a set amount in cash for your unrestricted use, usually $30 to $50 a day while you're in the hospital. At first glance, an advertisement promising you more than $1000 a month during hospitalization may sound appealing. But on a closer look, indemnity policies are usually poor consumer buys.

To start with, many don't pay from the first day of hospitalization. They may instead have a waiting period of seven days or more. Since most hospital stays last less than a week, you can see that your chance for collecting anything at all under the policy is statistically not too good. Other indemnity policies will pay from day one of hospitalization due to *injury* but only after five to seven days for illness. Next, many policies have an effective date of coverage six months or more after you start paying premiums. This is so that you can't buy the coverage and then go right into the hospital for a nonemergency procedure and still expect to collect the cash. Finally, indemnity policies are not cheap, considering their relatively limited benefits and statistically low chance of payout. Costs for one individual typically range from $10 to $15 per month if under age 35 to $15 to $20 if 65 or over.

The bottom line is that you should *never* rely on an indemnity policy as your only or primary health insurance. The benefits are too meager. (With daily hospital costs running $600 or more across the country, what good would a $50-a-day indemnity policy do you, even if it paid out from day one of hospitalization?) Nor should indemnity policies be confused with or, substitute for, disability insurance (discussed in Chapter 4), because a disability policy replaces a percentage of your actual income and is not dependent on hospitalization or other health care expenses. So don't fall for the clever advertising come-ons. In fact, look closely at such ads. One tip-off that the insurance offered may not be a good deal is if the ad notes in small print that the offer is not valid in California or New York, two states that regulate insurance sales in the consumer's interest very closely.

Dental insurance. This coverage has grown rapidly in recent years, mostly through large group plans. About 35 percent of employees enjoy some kind of dental insurance today. Dental coverage, however, is often limited in the services it will pay for—ordinary procedures such as fillings, extractions, and perhaps bridgework and dentures. The annual maximum amount payable is also often fairly limited—$500 to $600. Many dental policies won't pay for gum work, which is usually where the problem is for anyone over age 35. Some dental policies don't include coverage for braces and will pay for root canal work only under certain conditions. Cosmetic dentistry is excluded. Deductibles and 80 percent co-insurance usually apply. If you get dental insurance through your employer, fine. It's less readily available on an individual-plan basis, and it's relatively expensive given the limited coverage.

Dread disease (cancer) insurance. This is a bad consumer buy. It's usually sold through melodramatic print and TV ads that frequently employ celebrity spokespeople. Nor should you be fooled by the fact that some otherwise legitimate insurance companies offer cancer coverage. Mutual of Omaha, for example, sells an individual "dread" plan at $5.35 a month, available in most states to anyone under age 65. But think about that. It means that if you're 30, you'll pay as much as someone 60, although statistically you have a much lower chance of contracting the disease. With an additional *rider,* the Mutual of Omaha policy will pay $2500 upon diagnosis of internal cancer and up to $150,000 in further benefits. Sure, that money would come in handy if you developed cancer, but a comprehensive major medical policy would cover you not just equally but, in fact, more broadly.

Other insurers will sell you, for a few hundred dollars, a "dread disease rider" on your existing policy that pays if you're hospitalized for such things as rabies or tetanus—which, once again, would be covered under a good major medical. So do look at ads for cancer or dread disease insurance closely. Take note especially if the insurance is unavailable or severely restricted in New York, where regulators have determined that its sale is not in the consumer's best interest.

Women and Health Insurance

Women have some special concerns with regard to health insurance. To start with, they are more likely to experience a disruption in their health insurance coverage, due to divorce or widowhood, and the kinds of jobs in which many women are employed. If divorced, women frequently lose the health insurance coverage that was previously provided by their spouse. And women who are members of the part-time labor force or are in low-paying full-time jobs or in the service industry are less likely to be provided with health insurance by their employers. Moreover, women who try to obtain good individual coverage find they face higher costs than men and tougher health criteria for acceptance.

If you are a woman seeking a good health insurance package, you should first try to qualify for a group plan—generally, the larger the group, the better. If your employer does not offer such a plan, or if you are not employed, investigate getting coverage through other groups, such as religious, professional, trade, or alumni associations. The American Association of University Women, the National Organization of Women, and the Older Women's League, all headquartered in Washington, D.C., also offer group coverage to qualified women.

If you don't qualify as a member of any group offering advantageous health insurance rates, you must seek out individual coverage. In general, you should be prepared to pay more and get less. For example, the length and dollar amount of coverage for hospitalization are likely to be lower, and drugs and doctor visit coverage may be excluded or limited, as may be special treatments such as mental health, dental, and maternity care.

If divorce or widowhood threatens to remove you from coverage under your husband's group work plan, you may be able to convert your old group coverage to an individual policy if you pay a *conversion premium* directly to the insurer. Unfortunately, insurance under a conversion policy will probably not be available to you at the old group rate. For example, one divorced woman we know qualified for a conversion policy, but at a dramatically higher rate. Her husband's share of premium payments had previously been $72 a month for the entire family's coverage, but her individual conversion policy was priced at $225 monthly. (The average price of converting these benefits is between $175 and $225 a month.) And if you are unfortunate enough to have a preexisting condition, you may have to pay $4000 to $7000 for a conversion policy—if you can find one at all. So, while three-quarters of the states today have some kind of conversion law, that unfortunately doesn't translate into widely available, reasonably priced plans for the divorcée or widow. And a final point: Even if you can afford a conversion, you must work *fast*, since conversion privileges are usually good for only 30 days after your "regular" coverage has lapsed!

Better news is that Congress in 1985 passed a law requiring employers to offer health insurance at group rates to employees who have been fired or laid off. (This of course applies to men and women alike). *This is an exceedingly valuable right*, as it offers up to 36 months of coverage at your old group rate, plus a surcharge of 2 percent to cover administrative costs. Moreover, by law you are guaranteed coverage so long as the company gets your first premium payment within 105 days of your departure from the company.

Health Insurance and the New Tax Law

Under the new tax law, self-employed workers qualify for a new tax deduction beginning in 1987 to help subsidize the cost of their health insurance. If you work for yourself and have purchased a health insurance policy, you can now deduct 25 percent of the premium for coverage of yourself and dependents. (If you are an employee of an organization providing a health insurance plan, you've long enjoyed the benefit of fully excluding from taxes the health insurance paid for you by your employer. The new tax law does not change that.)

Otherwise, the new tax law makes it tougher to deduct itemized medical expenses. Beginning in 1987, out-of-pocket medical expenses will be deductible only to the extent they exceed 7.5 percent of your adjusted gross income —that's up from 5 percent under the old law. This will exclude an estimated nine million of the taxpayers who have been claiming the deduction from qualifying any longer, and will provide a smaller benefit for the remainder. So if you've been counting on the tax deduction to help offset some of your out-of-pocket medical expenses, you'd better review your health insurance policy to make sure it provides adequate coverage in light of the now reduced tax benefits.

Older Americans and Health Insurance

The elderly, too, have special problems with health insurance. Just at the time you're most likely to need it, adequate coverage can be hard to get—because you're retired or widowed, or simply because you're older and considered to be a poor insurance risk. That's why the federal government created Medicare in 1965. But as seniors across the country have learned, you rely exclusively on Medicare for health insurance today at your financial peril. Indeed, Medicare will generally cover less than half—some experts say less than a third—of your health care costs, and the fraction appears to be dropping annually. The gap in Medicare coverage can leave you with tens of thousands of dollars in unreimbursed medical bills in just a few months of serious illness. How do you protect yourself?

First, you need to understand what Medicare does and doesn't cover. Medicare coverage comes in two parts—Part A for hospitalization and Part B for medical services. Neither coverage is comprehensive. Part A has no premium but does have a deductible of $356. It pays for hospitalization for the first 60 days—but only what the government considers "reasonable and customary," which is not necessarily what the hospital actually charges. It includes coverage for a semiprivate room, meals, normal nursing services, intensive care, lab work and X rays, operating and recovery room, anesthesia, drugs, dressings, casts, and in-hospital therapy. After 60 days, you pay $89 a day for continued care until day 90; then, under a special once-in-a-lifetime 60-day reserve, you pay $178 a day until day 150. After 150 days, Medicare runs out, and all the costs are yours.

After three days in the hospital, Medicare A also qualifies you for 100 days in an eligible *skilled nursing facility*—20 days at full coverage, 80 days at partial. It also pays for an unlimited number of home nursing visits by skilled personnel. It's critical to understand that Medicare A doesn't pay for custodial (versus skilled) nursing care at an intermediate care facility—the kind of place where the majority of nursing home residents live.

Medicare B has a small monthly premium and a $75 deductible. It covers physician services, inpatient and outpatient medical services and supplies, physical and speech therapy, blood, and ambulance—subject to 20 percent co-insurance (exception: home health care is reimbursed at 100 percent). It doesn't cover dental care, eyeglasses, hearing aids, drugs, or long-term nursing care. And remember, you pay all charges that are higher than those approved by the government.

It's easy to see the gaps in this coverage—painfully so, in fact, after the first 150 days, or five months, of hospital care. For this reason, older Americans need *Medicare supplement policies* to help meet the cost of the patient's share of the bills. These are often referred to as "Medigap" policies. The bad news is that even the best of them rarely fill the gap.

There are many Medigap policies on the market. To begin to comparison-shop, ask your local Social Security office for a booklet called "Guide to Insurance for People with Medicare." Then ask a prospective insurer if the Medigap policy you're considering meets the minimum benefits recommended by the federal government for such policies. These minimum recommended benefits include coverage for your share of Part A hospital expenses from day 61 to day 90, as well as your 60-day reserve; coverage of 90 percent of Medicare-eligible expenses for an additional 365 days; a payment of at least $5000 a year to supplement Part B benefits; and a limit on the preexisting condition exclusion of six months. Remember, these are recommended *minimums*—you're not getting anything special or extra with a policy that offers these features.

Medicap policies are generally expensive, varying in cost, of course, by the exact benefits provided, the number and type of restrictions, and the age of the purchaser. And they still won't cover custodial nursing home costs—such as assistance with bathing, dressing, and eating—offered in intermediate care facilities. As a result, as many as thirty insurers today have moved to fill this particular gap by offering "intermediate care nursing" policies. Benefits vary widely, but generally the policies provide a $40 to $80 daily benefit for extended nursing home care below the skilled care level. These benefits generally last four to five years, with dollar caps ranging from a low of $36,000 to in excess of $200,000. Premiums vary dramatically with the specific benefits provided, the waiting period before benefits begin, the dollar cap, restrictions and age of the purchaser. They are available for as little as $120 from United Equitable, Lincolnwood, Illinois, to a "Cadillac" policy from AIG Life of New York City for $2550. (The "average" policy is in the $600 price range.) Expensive? Perhaps less so when you consider that the average annual per person cost for nursing home care in 1986 was $21,000

—with some homes costing up to $50,000. If you're considering such a policy for yourself or a loved one, check the following:

- Is coverage provided for mental disorders (senility, Alzheimer's)?
- Is there an age eligibility limitation?
- Can someone with an existing illness be covered?
- Does coverage apply only to posthospitalization or after a stay in a skilled nursing facility?
- Are some home-based health services covered?
- How long do benefits last? What is the dollar cap? Is the premium waived a certain time after benefits begin?

Be absolutely sure custodial care is covered, and not just care in a skilled nursing facility. Check with the American Association of Retired Persons (AARP) in Washington, D.C., which is itself test-marketing a long-term care policy. In addition, Aetna Life Insurance (203/273-3600), The Fireman's Fund (800/321-9352), and Prudential Insurance (212/307-1414) are among the commercial underwriters offering such policies today.

Shopping for Health Insurance

If you're among the one in seven Americans without health insurance, shopping for it should be a top priority. Similarly, if you have insurance but it provides only limited coverage, consider a supplemental policy.

- Ask your employer, friends, and others whose judgment you trust if they can recommend a health insurance company for your consideration. Or use the Yellow Pages to identify the major insurers (most of whom will be household names) that offer health insurance. In addition to Blue Cross/Blue Shield, these include, but are not limited to, Cigna, Liberty Mutual, New York Life, Mutual of Omaha, Metropolitan Life, New England Life, Prudential, State Farm, Transamerica Life, and The Travelers. Get quotes from a minimum of three companies for the same coverage—that is, the same set of benefits, inclusions, exclusions, waiting periods, deductibles, and co-insurance. You must compare like products to like for the comparison to be meaningful.
- Buy *comprehensive coverage*—Basic Protection plus Major Medical

—if you can possibly afford it. Your goal should be to cover at least 75 percent of the medical expenses of illness or injury. However, if you can't afford both Basic Protection and Major Medical, opt for the latter, with maximum benefits of at least $250,000 reinstated annually. This will at least protect you from the financial catastrophe a prolonged illness can bring.

- If possible, try to get coverage through a group. The benefits are usually more comprehensive, and group coverage can be half the cost of an individually purchased plan. If you're not eligible for a group plan at work, check out possibilities through a union, guild, fraternal organization, or alumni association. Some of the major insurers may offer only group plans, but they will try to work with you to develop a small group or to place you in an existing group.
- An *extension-of-benefits clause* is useful to have in your group plan because it will extend coverage for free for 30 days or more if you are fired or retired. Also seek at least a 31-day grace period during which you retain coverage if your premium payment is overdue.
- Look for a clear, comprehensive list of benefits. If it's not spelled out in the policy as a covered service, chances are it isn't reimbursable. Things often excluded are prescription drugs, alcoholism and mental health treatment, ambulances, and private-duty nursing, so look specifically for these. A good policy will provide for them— they are not too much to hope for. Read the fine print on waiting periods, exclusions, and limitations especially closely.
- Check to see if your plan includes coverage for *treatment away from home* in case you get sick while traveling and need the services of a physician or hospital elsewhere.
- If you don't qualify for group coverage, look to Blue Cross, which has open enrollment periods for Basic Protection, when you can enroll regardless of health status (there will be a waiting period for coverage of "preexisting" conditions). Commercial companies don't have open enrollment—they "select" their enrollees.
- Blue Cross is usually the best buy for individual basic protection plans, but not all "Blues" offer major medical to individuals, so you may have to go "commercial" for that. However, if you're a young couple who can afford a premium-reducing high deductible (generally not offered by Blue Cross), you might be better off buying all your coverage through a commercial firm.

- In any case, take the highest deductible you can manage (in an individually purchased policy, a minimum of $500) and co-insure 20 to 25 percent to keep premiums down.
- Look for a policy with an advantageous *family deductible,* a *deductible carryover* feature, and a *stop loss* limiting your total out-of-pocket expenses to a manageable level (generally $2500 to $5000).
- Look for a policy with a *high loss ratio,* which is the percentage of premiums paid and returned to clients as benefits. The higher the number, the better for you. Blue Cross plans should have loss ratios of 85 to 90 percent; commercial group plans, 80 to 90 percent; commercial individual plans (overhead is much higher), 60 percent or more. This applies to Medigap policies too.
- You want a policy that's *noncancelable* and *guaranteed renewable,* without regard to a change in health. Understand, however, that a policy that is guaranteed renewable *can* have its premiums increased, so long as they are increased for the whole group. A good group policy will not, however, increase its premiums every year, so it's useful to ask about the recent premium history.
- Choose a policy that pays *full-service* as opposed to inside-limits benefits. This is one reason not to rely on mail-order insurance as your main policy—it pays the latter. In fact, skip indemnity policies and dread disease policies—they're usually poor consumer buys. In general, watch out for mail-order insurance.
- With a comprehensive health insurance package, you generally don't need *riders;* they add unnecessary expense.
- Pay your premium annually or semiannually; it's cheaper.
- When you receive a policy, take advantage of the ten-day "free look," during which you can get a refund if you decide it's not right for you.
- Expect to pay $1750 to $3000 for comprehensive family coverage. If your policy costs much less, it probably isn't comprehensive and warrants study for possible supplementation.

Summary

If you already have a health insurance policy, use the guidelines provided in this chapter to analyze it. Understand the policy's components, how it pays benefits, deductibles, co-insurance, reasonable and customary limits and exclusions. These are essential to estimating your out-of-pocket medical expenses.

If you are one of the 37 million Americans without health insurance, shopping for a policy should be a top priority. If you can afford it, buy a comprehensive policy offering basic protection and major medical. If you can't afford both, opt for major medical to protect against the financial catastrophe a prolonged illness can bring.

Health insurance costs have skyrocketed in recent years, and employers are shifting more and more of the burden onto employees. If your employer announces any kind of change in your health plan, study it carefully. Look especially for financial incentives and penalties that are being built in to plans today. Your plan may have mandatory second opinions for surgery, or higher reimbursement for ambulatory surgery or generic drugs, for example. You need to know these things to use your health insurance plan in the most advantageous way.

If you are an older American, use the guidelines provided here to assess your coverage under Medicare and to supplement your policy cost effectively.

2

Alternative Health Care Plans

IN RECENT YEARS, INSURERS AND EMPLOYERS HAVE
DEVELOPED HEALTH CARE ALTERNATIVES AIMED AT
STEMMING THE NATION'S GROWING MEDICAL COSTS. MORE
THAN 25 MILLION U.S. CITIZENS ARE ENROLLED IN HMOs
AND PPOs, SAVING AN AVERAGE 25 PERCENT ON MEDICAL
EXPENSES.

IN LIGHT OF THEIR VIRTUAL ELIMINATION OF
DEDUCTIBLES AND CO-INSURANCE, HMOs AND PPOs,
COMPARED TO TRADITIONAL INSURANCE, MIGHT EASILY
SAVE YOU $500 TO $1000 OR MORE ON ONE MAJOR ILLNESS
ALONE.

Marketplace competition has come to the health care industry. With a substantial and growing glut of doctors and hospitals, it's increasingly a buyer's market for health care services. There's a lot of potential in this situation—which amounts to a radical restructuring of the industry—for you as a medical consumer, *if* you know how to decipher the new options available to you in both the provision of and payment for health care services. With an understanding of the basics, it's not that difficult. Let's start with HMOs.

What Is an HMO?

A friend of ours, Felicia M., had a baby this spring. She had both a complicated pregnancy requiring many extra tests and a difficult cesarian delivery. She and her baby girl stayed in the hospital for six days after the birth. But for all the medical treatment she received during the nine months, Felicia had out-of-pocket medical bills of $52. How? She's a member of Prucare, a prominent HMO in Houston owned by Prudential Insurance.

The "health maintenance organization" (HMO) is the best known of the alternative health care plans available today. An alternative to traditional health insurance and the usual fee-for-service (pay as you go) health care, it's an organization of health care professionals and facilities that provides comprehensive services to members for a fixed, prepaid monthly fee. In other words, it's both health insurance and the actual health care delivery system to its members. The monthly fee is paid directly to the HMO and is the same no matter how much (or how little) medical treatment one receives during the period. When a member does receive treatment at an HMO facility, there's no doctor, hospital, laboratory, or other medical bill, no matter how complex or lengthly the treatment, and there are no deductible or co-insurance payments to speak of. (Some HMOs charge a nominal $2 to $5 per visit.)

HMOs have been growing rapidly since the early 1980s. By 1986, more than 20 million Americans were enrolled in more than 430 HMOs across the country, up from 12 million enrolled in 270 HMOs in 1984. The explanation for this growth is largely that HMOs offer comprehensive, high-quality medical care at significant cost savings to both employers and insurers and to the members themselves. Experts predict continued explosive growth in HMO enrollment, with projections varying from 50 to 100 million enrollees by 1990.

HMOs can be either profit-seeking or nonprofit, and they have been founded by many groups: communities, employees, unions, universities, and insurance companies. (Blue Cross/Blue Shield is one of the largest purveyors of HMOs.) And today, more and more doctors and hospitals themselves—the providers of medical care—are forming HMOs in a self-defensive effort to protect their patient base and their overall business.

HMOs differ dramatically in size—in numbers of enrollees, participating physicians, clinical facilities, and affiliated hospitals. Some large HMOs even have their own hospitals. HMOs also differ in geographic scope. Many are strictly local, but many today are chains or networks that cross state lines.

Types of HMOs

There are basically two types of HMOs: prepaid Group Practice (GP) or Individual Practice Association (IPA). The former is the more common, enrolling substantially more than half of the nation's HMO members. In the GP model, care is provided primarily by physicians who are on the staff as full-time, salaried employees of the HMO or are members of an independent medical group on contract to the HMO. These doctors get the same salary, regardless of how many patients they see or procedures they perform. Ambulatory care is provided in a well-equipped, centrally located facility belonging to and used exclusively by the HMO. Certain local hospitals are affiliated with the HMO and are used for treatment requiring inpatient care.

The IPA model, in contrast, is one that contracts with physicians in individual practice to provide health services to HMO members. These doctors usually have non-HMO, or "private," patients, too; in effect, such doctors (maybe your own is already one) work part-time for the HMO. Care to the HMO enrollee, like the private patient, is provided in the individual doctor's office rather than at a central facility, with the HMO acting as the corporation or fiscal agent of the IPA. The physicians bill the HMO, on a previously agreed, usually modified fee-for-service basis. When hospital care is required, you go to one of the participating hospitals, where your bills are paid by the HMO.

What Health Services Are Provided by HMOs?

For the set monthly fee, you are eligible for comprehensive health care from HMO personnel and facilities. Basic benefits, which by federal law are both 100 percent covered (in the insurance sense) and directly provided by all HMOs, include the following:

- Physicians' services, including consultant and referral services
- Inpatient and outpatient hospital services
- Diagnostic, laboratory, and therapeutic radiology services
- Home health services

29

- Preventive health services
- Medically necessary emergency health services
- Short-term outpatient mental health services
- Medical treatment and referral service for alcohol or drug abuse

As you know from Chapter 1, these basic benefits are more comprehensive than those covered by traditional health insurance. For example, there is no limit on the number of covered days of necessary hospital care, nor on the number of doctor's office visits for an HMO participant. But the key difference between an HMO and traditional insurance is the HMO's coverage of *preventive care.* Just as its name indicates, the emphasis at HMOs is on *maintaining* your health. This is obviously in the HMO's interest (not to mention your own!), because it gets exactly the same amount of money each month whether you're well or ill. Illness exacts a financial toll on the HMO. So it provides and pays for preventive care: periodic physicals and checkups, Pap tests, eye and ear examinations, infant and child care, immunizations (our friend Felicia looks forward to practically no bills for her new baby's medical care), often preventive dentistry for children, and (in many HMOs) such counseling services as weight control, family planning, and hypertension screening. Because there's no charge (or only a nominal one) for these preventive services, there's little temptation to skimp on them. And with the emphasis on prevention, coupled with unlimited office visits, early diagnosis is often possible, because a member's concern about out-of-pocket costs is eliminated.

In addition to the basic benefits, many HMOs provide a range of supplemental benefits, available as riders to basic coverage, for such things as prescription drugs, facilities for intermediate or long-term care, physical and speech therapy, and dental and orthodontic care.

Be aware that there are some common *exclusions* to HMO coverage:

- Service not provided, authorized, or arranged by your HMO physician (For example, if you go to a doctor who does not practice with your HMO who sends you to the hospital for a nonemergency hernia repair operation, the HMO will not pay for the procedure or the hospital stay. For your medical care to be covered by your HMO membership, it must be authorized by your personal HMO physician and performed at an HMO-affiliated facility.)
- Conditions covered by workers' compensation or for which care is

reimbursable by a government agency (e.g., military service connected conditions)
- Cosmetic surgery
- Custodial care or long-term nursing home care
- Eyeglasses and hearing aids
- Whole blood or blood components
- Personal services and comfort and convenience items such as private hospital rooms and TV rentals
- Emergency service charges *in excess of* the usual and customary charge as determined by the HMO
- Experimental medical or other health services (such as *in vitro* fertilization)

What Is It Like to Go to an HMO?

Certainly the comprehensive approach to medical services and payment coverage offered by HMOs is appealing, but what is it like to go to one? Is it different from going to a "regular" doctor? Is it like a clinic? Do you make appointments or just walk in? Do you see a different doctor every time? What happens when the health center is closed?

First of all, even HMOs with centralized facilities are not like clinics—at least they should not and need not be. Nearly all the people visiting HMOs do so by *appointment.* However, whether HMO members must wait longer to get appointments than patients going to a fee-for-service doctor is the subject of some debate. Research conducted in the early 1980s indicated they did not. But a report released in August 1986 by the Rand Corporation, a major think tank that studied HMOs over a 13-year period at a cost of $80 million, suggested that HMO members *do* wait longer for appointments. However, once HMO patients have appointments and are in the doctor's office, studies show they are kept waiting about 18 minutes, versus about 20 minutes for "regular" doctors.

More important, an HMO is not like a clinic because members select a personal physician from among the HMO staff. So forget about the worry that you'll see a different doctor every time. You choose a personal primary care physician who is responsible for your *total health care* and is your first adviser on all health matters. He or she will either treat you directly or refer you to a staff (or, if necessary, outside) specialist. Each member of your family can designate a different personal physician—a woman might choose an ob-gyn and the man an internist, and they would choose a pediatrician for a baby or a child. If you choose a doctor and later decide you're not happy with your choice, you're free to select a new physician from among the HMO staff. You've got a lot of leeway there.

Do HMO doctors have too many patients? Are they overbooked so that you feel pressured to get in and out of the office as fast as possible? While HMOs differ in physician-patient ratios, just as fee-for-service practices do, the ratio *is* slightly lower in HMOs than the national average for fee-for-service practices. That is, HMO doctors, on average, do have more patients assigned to them than doctors in private practice. Still, available studies indicate that the time HMO physicians spend with each patient is within national norms. However, one way in which HMOs try to maximize the efficiency of doctors' time is by using other health personnel like nurse practitioners for preliminary or routine exams and procedures like blood pressure testing.

Finally, what about emergency care needed after the HMO health center is closed? No problem. A good HMO offers 24-hour access to medical attention. Doctors are always on call to see you or to instruct you on what to do and where to go. If an emergency is life-threatening, you should obviously have the option to go to the nearest medical facility, whether or not it's affiliated with the HMO. Generally, for the HMO to pay for services provided in that situation, you must notify the HMO promptly, within 48 hours. HMOs also cover out-of-town emergency care that is "medically necessary," which means that the need for services couldn't reasonably have been anticipated before leaving the HMO service area and that delay in obtaining the care would be a danger to your health. Again, you must notify your HMO promptly about such out-of-town emergency care to ensure HMO payment of its costs.

In some ways, going to an HMO may be better than going to a regular fee-for-service practice. An HMO provides centralized medical care (at least the more common group model does), with all medical services in one place, providing "one-stop shopping" convenience. Felicia, for example, plans to coordinate her visits to her obstetrician with her daughter's well-baby visits to the pediatrician. Many HMO facilities have on-site laboratories, diagnostic and radiology centers, other advanced equipment, and even pharmacies. What's more, with all your records in one place, you have a single chart with a complete medical record on it. Any staff doctor you're referred to has immediate access to this chart. This saves time and helps to minimize duplication of testing and services. Remember, too, that an HMO doctor has no financial incentive to overtreat, to order extra tests, and so on, because doing so generates no extra income for that doctor or for the HMO. (Under traditional health insurance, duplication of testing is very common. We know of a woman who was given three syphilis tests, of all things, during a three-day maternity stay!) Finally, a peer review system is built into the HMO organization; in the best HMOs, this can include chart audits, utilization review, hospital coordination and discharge planning, doctor referral review, and member grievance processes. In this way, the medical professionals at an HMO work as a team to provide continuous evaluation of the health care delivered to members. That's more than just a second-opinion safeguard for you!

Quality of Care

All these points relate to quality of care provided by HMOs, but there are more basic questions. How good are HMO doctors? Are HMOs staffed by second-best?

Not in the least. Several studies have shown that most HMO doctors are either board-certified or board-eligible in their fields. That means they meet high standards of training. And if you think about it, HMOs have a strong incentive to hire quality doctors, because if a doctor doesn't solve your health problem promptly and efficiently (if a misdiagnosis is made or treatment is delayed so that the condition worsens), you're just going to keep coming back until the problem is solved. You won't pay any more, but it certainly will cost the HMO more. For that reason, a second-rate physician is terribly expensive to an HMO.

It's easy to understand why HMOs want good doctors. But why would good doctors want an HMO? Wouldn't they prefer to be their own boss, with open-ended income potential, depending on how hard they wanted to work? Of course some would. But remember the growing glut of doctors. In 1965 there were 277,600 doctors in the United States, one for every 697 Americans. Today there are 506,000 doctors, or one for every 471 of us. By 1990 there will be 600,000, and a surplus estimated at between 70,000 and 185,000. It's no surprise, then, that the growth rate in doctors' incomes has slowed dramatically in recent years, as they compete with one another for patients. In fact, many physicians reported a drop in income of 10 to 40 percent in 1985 versus 1984. (One doctor joked along these lines that

M.D. used to stand for "Mercedes driver," but now it stands for "market-driven.")

A good, steady HMO salary, with predictable raises, can look pretty attractive in this context. In addition, HMOs pay their doctors' malpractice premiums, which can exceed $35,000 annually in the higher-risk specialties like obstetrics. You have to see quite a large number of patients just to pay premiums at that level. Moreover, HMO doctors don't have the administrative hassle and overhead of running an office. Another plus is that they have predictable hours—important to many young doctors who are part of two-career families and place strong emphasis on their home life. Finally, with medical school costs so high, the average graduate begins practice with a $30,000 debt, making financing a new private practice difficult.

For these reasons, young doctors in particular are flocking to HMOs. An American Medical Association survey showed that 39 percent of doctors under age 36 are employees rather than self-employed, versus only 19 percent over age 56. And a 1985 nationwide survey conducted by Lou Harris pollsters showed that 46 percent of physicians were at least considering affiliation with an HMO, a far cry from the early days when many doctors considered HMOs "socialized medicine."

One young HMO physician explained to us, "If I wanted to run a business, I'd have gone to Harvard Business School. I wanted to practice medicine, but I also wanted to be home by seven o'clock for dinner and to help with the kids. I didn't have the money to invest in a private practice, and, just as important, I didn't have the time. I love my work, but I don't want to be a slave to it. An HMO is the perfect solution."

So it becomes easy to understand why very prominent HMOs sometimes get 1000 applications for a single staff opening. But are these good doctors "free" to practice the best medicine in an HMO? What about the concern that an HMO might skimp on medical care, since to treat patients and, especially, to hospitalize them costs the HMO money without producing any additional income? This is a serious concern, and those who express it sometimes cite the fact that HMO members are hospitalized over a third less frequently than people with traditional health insurance. Critics of HMOs cite this as indication that HMOs yield to the financial temptation to "under-treat."

The quality of HMO care has been much studied. No research we're aware of concludes that HMOs skimp on medical care or provide lower-quality care than traditional fee-for-service practices. In 1980, for example, researchers at Johns Hopkins University determined after extensive study that "there is little question that HMO care is at least comparable to care in other health care facilities, if not superior." Even more interesting is the study published by an American Medical Association (AMA) group. As the AMA has maintained an officially "neutral" stance with regard to the HMO concept, their conclusion is all the more compelling: "The medical care delivered by HMOs appears to be of a generally high quality. . . . The HMO approach, where viable, appears to have the potential to provide health care of acceptable quality at a lower total cost to enrollees than many other health care systems." And, the AMA study added, "nothing in the literature indicates that HMO savings result from enrollees receiving less care than they need."

Then why are HMO members hospitalized less frequently? Because HMOs frequently substitute outpatient care for hospitalization. Since traditional health insurance still often covers more of the bill if work is done in the hospital rather than a doctor's office, fee-for-service doctors have a tendency to hospitalize patients for some minor surgical procedures and tests. Private physicians have also been forced to practice ultraconservative, defensive medicine in light of skyrocketing medical lawsuits and jury awards. Moreover, doctors affiliated with hospitals know that occupancy rates are down and that hospitals are making less or even losing money, so they sometimes recommend hospitalization in a marginal situation to help out. But HMO doctors have the opposite incentive. The patient doesn't pay more in either case, but it costs the HMO much more to hospitalize someone. Hence there's a strong incentive to perform procedures that lend themselves to it on an outpatient basis. Since it's estimated that 20 to 40 percent of all surgery —as many as 275 different procedures—can be performed safely on an outpatient basis, and at roughly a 50 percent savings, it's easy to see why many health analysts see HMOs as a major cost-containment development in health care. The Department of Health and Human Services has estimated that by 1988, increasing use of HMOs may save $20 billion in hospital costs alone.

But there is a final word on the quality-of-care debate. The same 1986 Rand study cited earlier noted that 15 percent of the HMO enrollees studied were *dissatisfied* with their care, not just because of long waits for appointments but, more important, because of a perceived reduced availability of hospital care and specialists. Thus the very cost-cutting methods that make HMOs attractive from an economic point of view appear from one major study to increase patient dissatisfaction with their medical care. Although we have many friends who are HMO members and delighted with the care they receive, at least one friend, Kathy V., quit her New York HMO because she "felt second-opinioned to exasperation."

Availability and Eligibility

It's pretty easy to find an HMO today. Many of the country's 430 HMOs are rapidly adding staff, facilities, and membership, and new HMOs are being started all the time. However, one estimate has it that almost half of all Americans live in areas still not served by HMOs. In general, HMOs tend to be concentrated in and around major urban areas or in areas of rapid population growth and mobility. A main reason for this is that an HMO needs a fairly substantial number of members to be economically viable. HMOs also seem to do best in places where there are a lot of newcomers who don't have existing ties to specific doctors. These people can enroll in an HMO with confidence about the general quality of care and avoid having to shop around for a good doctor. In contrast, in small, rural communities, people are more likely to have a long-time family doctor from whom they don't want to break to try something new. Today, HMOs are strongest in California, Washington, Oregon, New York, Massachusetts, Hawaii, Florida, Minnesota, and certain rapidly growing areas in the South. In Minneapolis–St. Paul, for example, as many as 80 percent of physicians are affiliated with one of the area's HMOs, and 40 percent of the population are HMO-enrolled. In San Francisco, one-third of the population is enrolled in HMOs; in Los Angeles and Portland, one-quarter. In other major cities in these states, it's common to find one-fifth of the population as HMO enrollees. So if you're interested in an HMO, you have an excellent chance of finding one if you live in or around a major urban area. HMOs advertise heavily. If friends or colleagues aren't able to steer you to one in your community, look in the Yellow Pages, skim the advertising sections of your newspaper or city magazines, or call the medical referral services most larger communities have nowadays.

Who is eligible to join? Requirements vary by HMO, although a few stipulations are held in common. First, you must live in an HMO's service area. Second, the majority of HMO members enroll through their employers. So another good source (probably the best) for information on HMO availability is the Employee Relations or Human Resources department at your place of work. Today, under federal law, an employer must offer employees the option of enrolling in a qualified HMO if the employer has at least 25 full or part-time employees living within the HMO's service area, contributes to a current health benefit plan, pays the minimum wage, and receives a written request from an area HMO. Moreover, your employer's contribution to HMO coverage must at least equal the amount contributed to your current health plan. If your company pays only part of your premiums in an existing health plan and you pay the rest by payroll deduction, your employer must make a similar payroll deduction available to you for your share of an HMO premium. Finally, if your employer offers certain separate, supplemental health benefits, such as prescription drugs, optical benefits, and group dental plans, and these services are not provided by the HMO open to you, your employer must provide you with continued eligibility for these supplemental benefits.

Most HMOs will allow you to convert a former employer-provided plan into an individual agreement if you terminate employment or lose coverage through divorce or attainment of the limiting age (that is, when a child reaches the age at which coverage is no longer provided under a parent's plan). Like traditional insurance, the cost will be higher for the individual coverage than it was for group.

What if you're not eligible to join an HMO through an employer (as when, for example, you're self-employed or your employer doesn't contribute to an existing health plan for you)? Do HMOs accept single applications? Many do, but some do not. Of those that do, it's usually only during a designated open-enrollment period. In other words, you may not be able to join at just any time that suits you. The only way to learn if (and when) HMOs in your service area accept single applications is to telephone and ask them.

The open-enrollment stipulation also sometimes applies to people joining HMOs through their employers. Perhaps you currently have a traditional health insurance plan through your employer but would like to switch to an HMO. You'll probably have to wait until the next open-enrollment period, which may come only once a year. It's different if you're a new employee or an employee just eligible for health coverage. In that situation, if your employer has an existing contract with an HMO, you're eligible to join immediately.

Finally, many HMOs have a "health qualifier" of one sort or another for enrollment. If you try to enroll in an HMO with certain preexisting conditions, you may not be eligible to join until that condition has passed. Or you may be allowed to join but not be provided with coverage for that particular condition. Diabetes and pregnancy are examples of preexisting conditions for which some HMOs will not provide coverage. Some HMOs are more liberal about preexisting conditions than others. In any case, you must, without fail, reveal such preexisting conditions on your HMO application or enrollment form.

HMO Fees

HMOs vary in the monthly fees or premiums they charge. A key variable is membership size. Larger HMOs, offering economies of scale, tend to be less expensive. HMOs also charge different fees for someone enrolling through a prepaid group plan and an individual or single contract. Finally, of course, rates vary according to the benefits provided. Everybody gets offered the basic benefits package, but supplemental benefits like dental coverage are separately negotiated and obviously entail additional cost.

The fees HMOs charge must be compared to those of traditional health insurers. Throughout the 1970s, it was commonly thought that HMO premiums were higher than those of the major insurance companies. However, according to a 1983 survey published by the Group Health Association of America, average HMO premiums for major groups have dropped below the premiums charged by traditional carriers in the early 1980s. As a rule, most HMOs today are cheaper than traditional health insurance. This is all the more the case because HMO benefits are also broader.

As of December 1985 HMO premiums averaged about $200 per month for family coverage and about $74 for single contracts provided through major group accounts. Comparable up-to-date figures for traditional health insurance premiums are not available, but are roughly estimated at 10 to 15 percent higher, while benefits are fewer. Since employers pay the biggest part of the nation's health insurance bills, it's easy to see why they're more and more interested in the HMO option. Some employers are even promoting HMOs by paying a bigger part of HMO premiums than they pay for traditional insurance, because they save money when employees opt for HMOs.

So HMOs can save your employer money; what about you? The answer for most people is that membership in an HMO will reduce overall out-of-pocket medical expenditures. The reduction can be substantial in some situations. One major study indicates that HMO members' overall out-of-pocket health care costs average 10 to 40 percent lower than those of people covered by traditional insurance. Another study put the figures at 20 to 25 percent.

To see how much money you might save by enrolling in a HMO, figure out your current health care costs, by adding any insurance premium payments you make, together with all your out-of-pocket costs resulting from deductibles, co-insurance, reasonable and customary fee limits, and excluded services. With an HMO, in contrast, there are virtually no out-of-pocket expenses. So, even if your HMO does charge a higher fee than the standard insurance premium, and even if you're required to pay a significant part, or all, of that HMO fee, your overall medical bill might still be lower in an HMO versus a traditional plan. In the instance where you pay part of your premium for traditional insurance and then switch to an HMO with lower monthly fees, your employer must still contribute to the HMO the same dollars that were contributed to traditional insurance. So in that situation, the amount you yourself pay in premiums would be reduced, perhaps even eliminated. Let's look at a specific example.

Before Felicia M. enrolled in Prucare, she was covered by traditional health insurance provided by her employer. Because she works in the Human Resources department at her company, Felicia is quite well informed about employee benefits such as comparative health coverage. So when she and her husband decided to start a family, they purposely switched out of the traditional health plan and into an HMO to save money. Table 2.1 shows the comparison they ended up with.

Preferred Provider Organizations

We've seen how HMOs have been both a response to and a catalyst for increasing competition in the financing and delivery of the nation's health care. HMOs have challenged the traditional "pay as you go" funding system that for years has subsidized the oversupply of doctors and hospitals. In the process, HMOs are saving the nation, insurers, employers, and individual consumers money.

The health care cost containment movement that HMOs have done so much to nurture has spawned another entrant into the health care delivery and financing system. The *preferred provider organization* (PPO) is a group of health care providers who have contracts with employers, insurers, or other third-party payers to deliver health care services to employee groups at reduced rates. These providers are "regular" doctors and hospitals that accept "regular" patients too, but they are willing (even eager) to discount prices to big insurance groups in exchange for the stable, high-volume business they bring in.

Table 2.1 Comparison of Maternity Costs Under a Traditional Insurance Plan and Through an HMO.

Actual Expenses		Traditional Insurance Insurance Reimbursement		HMO Out-of-Pocket Expenses
Obstetrician fee (cesarian)	$ 1750	Reasonable and customary fee	$ 1600	$24 ($2 per visit for 12 visits to obstetrician)
		Deductible	− 250	
			1350	
		Co-insurance	× 80%	
		Benefit paid	$ 1080	
Prenatal lab work	$ 60	Fee	$ 60	
		Co-insurance	× 80%	100% covered
		Benefit paid	$ 48	
Genetic counseling	$ 125	Not covered		100% covered
Vitamin prescription	$ 48	Not covered		100% covered
Stress tests	$ 150	Fee	$ 150	
		Co-insurance	× 80%	100% covered
		Benefit paid	$ 120	
Hospital charges	$ 3200	Charge	$ 3200	
		Deductible	− 250	100% covered
		Benefit paid	$ 2950	
Pediatrician fees (first-year well-baby visits and immunizations)	$ 280	Not covered		$16 ($2 per visit)
Total expenses	$ 5613	Total insurance reimbursement	$ 4198	
Total out-of-pocket	$ 1415			$40

It works like this: An insurance company will go to a group of hospitals and doctors who have formed a PPO for the purpose of contract bidding and ask for a bid on the business that insurance company is prepared to bring in. The bid is a pledge to provide a wide range of services—from hospital beds to appendectomies—at a fixed fee, discounted from the regular rates. (If the PPO actually performs the contracted-for service for less money than the bid, the difference is the PPO's "profit.") The insurance company encourages its plan members with financial incentives to use the facilities of whichever PPO wins the bid.

Winning bids are sometimes 25 percent or more off customary prices. For example, the largest PPO in the country, offered by Blue Cross of California, contracts with 21,000 doctors at 224 hospitals and has about 1 million enrollees. Its premium costs are 34 percent below standard insurance rates for the same benefits. It's easy to see why PPOs have caught the attention of insurers.

PPOs are also especially good for employers who have decided to self-fund their employee health care programs, usually due to disenchantment with ever-increasing traditional health insurer rates. Ameritrust, for example, recently successfully offered a PPO option to its employees. Its traditional health insurance program costs Ameritrust $1148 per person, whereas this new PPO costs only $742. So they can afford to offer their employees financial incentives to choose PPO services.

There are also a few purely "administrative" PPOs around. These don't provide actual medical services but rather negotiate their provision at reduced rates. In other words, they function as purchasing agents, bringing buyers and sellers together. Some say they can negotiate rates 20 percent off the standard fare. They make their money by charging the payers (insurance companies or employers who self-fund their programs) for the negotiating service.

As to how to find a PPO, your employer basically does it for you. PPOs are really only interested in big accounts. They go to the major insurers who provide the plans for employers, and the insurers sell these companies or unions on offering the PPO option to their employee or member groups. Your Employee Relations department or union representative will let you know whether your existing health plan has a PPO option or if one is under development.

PPOs Versus HMOs

PPOs and HMOs are similar in that they both challenge the traditional health insurance system under which the payers stand passively on the sidelines, wait for the bills to come in, and pay them. HMOs and PPOs actually *intervene* in the health care delivery system and, in effect, help make decisions about a patient's care. As systems, they try to insist that care is provided in the most cost-efficient way.

A PPO is somewhat like an HMO in that it allows the organizations that pay for health care, largely the big insurers, to contract directly with and in advance for services with the providers of the care, namely, doctors and hospitals. PPOs differ from HMOs, however, in that like traditional insurers, they generally operate on the principle of *benefit reimbursement;* they are *not* prepaid plans. What makes the PPO a twist on traditional insurance is that the PPO rewards prudent medical purchasing with a higher benefit. This is the way in which a PPO "intervenes" in the health care delivery system. Because of its quick access to data on charges from a wide array of hospitals, doctors, and laboratories, the PPO can make sure that care of all kinds is being delivered in the most cost-effective way. That keeps the providers *and* the consumers on their toes.

PPOs and the Medical Consumer

So how does the PPO work from the individual consumer's point of view?

First, PPOs were developed in part because of what some people saw as the restrictions of HMOs—the fact that the consumer must draw from a relatively small number of HMO physicians and hospitals or else pay the *entire* medical bill personally. PPOs, in contrast, offer a wider range from which to choose. If your insurer has contracted with PPO facilities, you can still choose to use a doctor or hospital that isn't part of the PPO system and receive reimbursement, but not to the same extent of coverage as you'd get if you'd chosen the PPO. There's an economic incentive built in to get you to choose lower-cost PPO services. Often it's the elimination of the deductible and/or co-insurance. Sometimes it's a substantial *increase* in the co-insurance factor—50 percent or more—if you don't go PPO. The insurer has negotiated a substantial savings with a PPO and has incentive to pass some of that on to you so that you will choose PPO services. So the bottom line is that the PPO option will save you out-of-pocket medical dollars.

PPOs are currently the fastest-growing option in health care coverage. From fewer than a dozen in the early 1980s, there are now about 125 PPOs in operation around the country. Where are they drawing their patients from? A study of the largest PPO indicates that 24 percent of enrollees switched from HMOs, while a whopping 76 percent switched from "regular" fee-for-service practices—once again indication of a trend favoring alternative medical delivery systems.

42

Managed Medical Systems

With HMOs and PPOs alike, the traditional line between provider and payer of health care is increasingly blurred. Experts expect them to look more and more alike in the years ahead, as new hybrid systems develop to draw on the advantages of each.

The *managed medical system* (MMS) is the current such hybrid. Although the MMS is a prepayment arrangement, like the HMO, it tries to take the best aspects of both the HMO and the PPO. The MMS has been called "prepayment with a choice" or "an HMO with an escape clause."

Like the HMO, the MMS holds the doctors and hospitals responsible for providing quality care at a reasonable cost. But it also has a mandatory, strict utilization control program that was earlier described as in place at only the best HMOs. Costly, inefficient medical practices stand less chance of persisting in an MMS than they do even in an HMO.

As with a PPO, a patient can choose a doctor outside the group and still have insurance coverage, though less of it. The "price" of choosing non-MMS facilities is a large deductible and increased co-insurance. Provider groups—mostly hospitals—and insurers are usually the sponsors of MMSs.

The MMS is still quite new and not very common. Like a PPO, you don't find an MMS; it finds you, through an employer-offered option under an existing health care plan. Again, ask your employee relations department or union representative if an MMS is in the offing.

Table 2.2 summarizes and compares how the three major types of health care plans—traditional insurance, HMOs, and PPOs—work.

Drawbacks of HMOs and PPOs

HMOs and PPOs have been found to offer high-quality, comprehensive health care at a cost savings. But that doesn't mean there are no drawbacks. First, there's the question of doctor selection. To put yourself in the care of an HMO, you'll have to sever relationships with your present physicians to get financial reimbursement; in a PPO, you can stick with your own doctor, but if your doctor is not affiliated with the PPO, you'll face a financial penalty from your insurer.

A related point is a concern about less personalized service, the most common complaint about HMOs. Our friend Kathy V. and others have also

43

Table 2.2 How Major Health Care Plans Work

	Standard Health Insurance[a]	Health Maintenance Organization	Preferred Provider Organization
Premium/rating[b]	Insurer sets premium on basis of degree of coverage, experience rating of group.	Prepaid plan, communitywide experience rating.	Negotiated premium, usually discounted. Covered-group experience rating.
Payment to providers	Based on policy of usual, customary, and reasonable fees. Deductible generally involved.	Physicians are salaried employees of HMO or are paid flat fee per patient per month. Usually no deductible.	Fixed fee at discounted rates under terms of PPO agreement. Little or no deductible.
Type of coverage	Varies with type of plan; the more comprehensive the coverage, the higher the premium.	Comprehensive coverage emphasizing preventive care.	Varies. Benefits can be tailored to each covered group.
Choice of provider	Patients may seek care from any physician or other provider who qualifies under plan.	Patients limited to providers employed by HMO.	Patients have financial incentive to use "preferred" provider but may choose not to and pay any charge differentials.
Type of medical practice	Physicians may be independent practitioners or part of group practice, but basis is fee for service in either case.	Participating physicians often practice in same location as part of multispecialty group within HMO. (Physicians who are members of independent practitioner associations continue their independent practices in addition to treating members of an IPA plan.)	Participating physicians may or may not practice in same location.

[a]Commercial health insurance and the nonprofit Blue Cross and Blue Shield plans.
[b]The rating is a measure of the extent to which a group of individuals covered by a plan use benefits of that plan. Premiums are based on the rating.
Source: Adapted from Clearinghouse on Business Coalitions for Health Action, U.S. Chamber of Commerce.

complained of their HMOs' tendency first to try simple and inexpensive "down-home" remedies and only later move on to more sophisticated and expensive treatment for problems such as infertility. Participating HMO doctors, ever watchful about utilization review, try to make doubly sure that they're prescribing the least costly treatment. It's been the experience of some patients that their HMO or PPO doctors hesitate to initiate treatment until it's crystal clear that the treatment is necessary and therefore an unavoidable expense to the organization. All in all, the Rand study showed that the patients who were "very satisfied" with their HMO care dropped from 57 percent in 1980 to 48 percent in 1984. (At the same time, however, those satisfied with their traditional insurance and pay-as-you-go medical services dropped from 53 percent to 34 percent. What these statistics really suggest is that medical consumers are simply becoming more demanding in their health care expenditures.)

How to Judge an HMO or PPO

As we've said repeatedly, HMOs and PPOs are alternatives to traditional, open-ended insurance funding systems for health care. However, HMOs and PPOs take different approaches. If you join an HMO, you leave traditional health insurance behind and go on a prepayment plan. With a PPO, arranged by your insurer-employer, you stay with the traditional insurance plan principle of benefit reimbursement, the twist being that your insurer will reward you with bigger benefits if you choose PPO facilities. Clearly, then, switching to an HMO is the more radical departure and requires the more careful comparison shopping. So the following observations focus more on HMOs.

- In considering an HMO, understand exactly what you'd be giving up in your traditional insurance plan in terms of benefits and costs so that you can make a meaningful comparison with potential HMOs. Be sure to understand if your existing plan offers, or is planning to offer, a PPO option. If so, it may be cheaper to stick with the traditional insurance and avail yourself of PPO facilities. Next, investigate whether and how you can get back into the traditional plan if you find that an HMO isn't right for you. You can usually switch back, but only during an open enrollment period, probably with exclusions for preexisting conditions.

- Ask about the HMO or PPO hospitalization rate. If hospital days per 1000 members are between 350 and 500, you can be reasonably sure that the HMO or PPO has a commitment to efficiency and economy that will work to keep premiums down over time.
- With an HMO, check on benefits offered in addition to the set basic benefits. Ask particularly about dental care, prescription drugs, and physical therapy. Make sure you understand any restrictions or limitations on these supplemental benefits (for example, preventive dentistry for children *up to age six*).
- Thoroughly check out the cost of the HMO, even if your employer will be picking up all or much of the monthly fee. At what rate has the HMO fee been increasing in recent years? Are there any out-of-pocket expenses?
- What hospitals are the HMO or PPO associated with? Do they have a good reputation in the community?
- If the HMO is of the "group practice" type, with centralized health facilities, make sure they're open for appointments a minimum of 40 hours a week. It's a nice plus if they offer appointment hours certain evenings and Saturdays.
- It's essential that an HMO offer around-the-clock medical emergency care. Ask about the "on-call" procedure for use when the health center is closed.
- Ask about the qualifications of the HMO or PPO doctors. Hope to learn that all or most of them are board-certified or at least board-eligible.
- Check out the overall fiscal health of the HMO (16 have failed in recent years, commonly because of inadequate membership growth, overstaffing or understaffing, setting fees too low, and poor location). Ask if the HMO is a member of the Group Health Association of America, as that will give you some indication of financial soundness. Be sure the HMO you're considering carries insolvency insurance, which would provide you with coverage should the HMO fail. Look for a clause in the HMO contract that holds individuals harmless for medical bills in the event of HMO failure.
- With a PPO, understand exactly the financial incentives your insurer has built into the program. Understand, too, the penalties for using medical facilities outside the PPO.

Summary

HMOs, PPOs, and MMSs represent real departures in the financing and delivery of health care in our society. They have injected into the medical system an important element of competition that offers many medical consumers an opportunity to receive high-quality care at lower cost. You owe it to yourself to consider these alternative health care plans. The following key points should be kept in mind:

- An HMO is both your health insurance and the actual health care delivery system. For a set, prepaid monthly fee you get comprehensive care with far fewer exclusions than under traditional health insurance and virtually no out-of-pocket costs from deductibles, co-insurance, or reasonable and customary fee limits.
- Studies show that HMOs generally compare favorably in terms of quality of care with fee-for-service medicine.
- Most people enroll in HMOs through their employers. However, for those of you without employer-provided health plans, many HMOs accept single applications.
- On average, it's estimated that an HMO will save you 25 percent in out-of-pocket medical expenses.
- A PPO is a group of health care providers who have contracts with employers or insurers to deliver health care services to employee groups at reduced rates. So to take advantage of a PPO, you have to be part of a larger employer group. The PPO option is negotiated for you by your employer.
- Employers generally won't force you to use PPO hospitals or doctors, but they will offer you a financial incentive for doing so. Usually, they'll reduce or waive deductibles and/or co-insurance. Because PPOs save them money, employers and insurers want you to use the PPO arrangement and will reward you with higher benefits for doing so. In other words, they pass some of the savings on to you.
- As with everything else, there are good and bad HMOs and PPOs. Use the guidelines provided in this chapter to evaluate any alternative health care plan you're considering.

3

Life Insurance

ALTHOUGH TWO-THIRDS OF ALL AMERICANS HAVE LIFE INSURANCE, THE MAJORITY HAVE LESS THAN HALF THE COVERAGE THEY NEED.

AMERICANS BOUGHT MORE THAN $1 TRILLION IN NEW LIFE INSURANCE COVERAGE IN 1985, YET ONLY ONE IN FIVE COMPARISON-SHOPPED FOR A POLICY.

In other words, not only are our families inadequately covered, but we're not protecting ourselves as consumers in the coverage we do purchase.

Life insurance is a critical part of total coverage. If there's anything we need to get really right to protect our families, it's life insurance. And if ever we need to be on guard as consumers, it's as purchasers of life insurance policies. But as technical and troublesome a topic as it may at first seem, if you spend just a few hours to learn the basics, you can make good, cost-effective decisions.

What Should Life Insurance Do?

The main purpose of life insurance is to protect dependents from the financial consequences of the death of a breadwinner. When you think life insurance, think *death benefits*. This is the essential perspective. Life insurance creates an "instant estate" for your family at your death. This instant estate steps in to replace part of the income you would have generated over the years had you continued to live.

Life insurance payouts are not subject to federal or state taxes. Your survivors may use these proceeds as they see fit: for immediate needs, such as burial and estate taxes; as intermediate income for a period of adjustment so that a spouse can regain independence; or for longer-term needs such as a college education for the children. Although life insurance agents frequently maintain that a policy has purposes other than financial protection for one's dependents—for example, as a forced savings or investment plan or a tax shelter—the real purpose is family financial protection in the event of untimely death of a breadwinner. As an insurance consumer you're less likely to be bamboozled into buying something you don't need if you keep death benefits foremost in mind.

Who Needs Life Insurance?

Not everyone. If you have no dependents, you have no need for life insurance. If you are a married couple, both working in well-paying jobs, it may be that neither of you needs to buy a policy (particularly if your employers provide you with some coverage at the office). However, if you are a primary breadwinner with one or more dependents, you almost certainly do need a life insurance policy.

An income earner plus one or more people who depend on that breadwinner for support create a compelling need for life insurance. A spouse who, for whatever reason, could not be self-supporting creates a need for life insurance. Perhaps the most compelling need, however, is created by a child. With only rare exceptions, the birth of a baby—who will require support for 18 or more years—creates the need for insurance on the life of the family's primary provider.

What if both members of a couple are breadwinners? In the absence of a child, perhaps neither would need life insurance, or at least not a substantial amount. It depends largely on whether either one could be self-supporting in a satisfactory manner in the other's absence. However, with the birth of a child, the situation changes, particularly if one of the adults (usually the mother) decides to stay home. Suddenly, what was a two-income, no-dependents couple becomes a threesome depending on one income into the foreseeable future—a situation that cries out for life insurance on the remaining provider.

When both adults continue as vital sources of family support after the birth of a child—increasingly common today—both should have life insurance, if possible. Their life insurance policies should be in rough proportion to their contribution to overall family income. If one adult earns substantially more than the other, the primary income earner needs the bigger life insurance policy. Let's emphasize this: The family priority should be to get the primary breadwinner adequate insurance—and "adequate" may be considerably more than you think, as we'll soon see—before buying insurance on the family's secondary provider.

Since more than half of all women are continuing to work outside the home today after the birth of a baby and contributing vital economic support to their families, you'd expect statistics to show a big jump in the number of women life insurance policyholders. They do. In 1971, the ratio of men to women policy buyers was 2.5 to 1. In 1981, it was 1.5 to 1—and the average-size policy purchased on women's lives has been increasing at a faster rate than that of men.

In fact, of course, a woman need not be a member of the paid work force to need or want a life insurance policy. These days, an increasing number of full-time homemakers have life insurance policies too. After all, a full-time homemaker makes a vital contribution to the economic well-being of the family. If the homemaker should die, especially if there are still young children in the house, these services would have to be replaced, and that would create a new and considerable cash outflow for the household. So life insurance on a full-time homemaker can be a good idea. There are several ifs, however. First, the breadwinner should be adequately insured before thought is given to homemaker insurance. Second, can the family afford a second insurance policy? If you're just starting out and money is especially tight, you probably have higher priorities, and homemaker insurance may be something you'll want to forgo. And third, if a family has savings or other income to pay for housekeeping and child care expenses in the event of the homemaker's death, it may not need homemaker insurance.

Should You Buy Life Insurance on Your Children?

The answer is no! It rarely, if ever, makes economic sense to do so. Resist the blandishments of life insurance agents—who usually start to call as soon as the birth announcement appears in the newspaper—who want to sell insurance on your baby's life. Remember that the main purpose of life insurance is to protect dependents from the financial consequences of a family provider's death, and you'll agree that it's not very sensible to carry a policy on a child.

Life insurance agents will argue that coverage for a child can be had at extremely low rates, so why not have it? The reason that the rates are so low is that, statistically, there's an exceedingly small chance that a growing child will die, requiring the insurance company to pay off. Agents will also argue that coverage bought for a young child guarantees later insurability as an adult, regardless of health. In fact, only about 3 percent of life insurance applicants are ever denied coverage for health reasons. So the answer remains an emphatic no. Life insurance for children is unnecessary and wasteful.

How Much Life Insurance Do You Need?

In researching this book, we found people with young dependents and no life insurance, others with small $10,000 policies, and a New York doctor with $3 million in coverage! It's safe to generalize that all of these choices are wrong.

The basic question you have to ask is, how much *income* would a surviving spouse with one or two young children need in the event of the death of the primary breadwinner? This, of course, is a highly personal question, as it's based in large part on your lifestyle and family financial goals. However, a tip-off to the fact that most of us are underinsured is found in a recent study showing that one widow in four uses her entire life insurance benefit within 60 days!

Life insurance rarely has to shoulder the burden of income replacement alone. Most of us have other income sources that come to the fore in the event of a breadwinner's death. You must first figure how much income these *other sources* would provide before you can determine how much life insurance the family needs.

First, there are Social Security *survivor benefits.* The families of most wage and salary earners working in jobs where Social Security taxes are paid are eligible. For those with substantial earnings, the benefits may be a significant start—up to about $1050 a month—and they are tax-free under the new tax law if your adjusted gross income is less than $25,000. A good life insurance agent can help you figure out what your family's Social Security survivor benefits would be, or you can get instructions from your local Social Security office and figure them out yourself. Survivor benefits are paid monthly, but they must be applied for—they don't start automatically. And it's important to note that these benefits are to a large degree *child-raising* benefits. They continue until the youngest child reaches age 18, or 22 if the child is a full-time student. After that, the surviving parent generally will not receive further survivor benefits until the age of 65. This "blackout period" must be part of your insurance planning.

Next, does the breadwinner have a group life insurance policy through work? About 56 percent of companies provide this benefit (down, unfortunately, from 63 percent in 1979). If so, in what amount? A year's salary is common. Does the employer also offer a *family income-protection program*? Some companies provide that an employee's survivors receive a certain percentage of that employee's last monthly income for a period of years equal to or double the employee's years on the job. Is the breadwinner also eligible for a pension or annuity or a member of a deferred compensation plan (including a veteran's pension) that is available in whole or in part to survivors?

Next, what cash and savings are available? Are there stocks or other investments? Is there equity in real estate or a business that would be sold in the event of the family provider's death? Finally, would the surviving spouse work outside the home for pay? What are the likely earnings? Going through this exercise will give you at least a rough estimate of the income that would be available in the event of the main breadwinner's death. Compare the results of this exercise with a general rule used by insurance experts:

- A surviving parent of two children usually needs 60 to 70 percent of the family's current after-tax income to maintain economic well-being.

If you've calculated that your family *would* have that much income—which is possible if Social Security benefits are available, if the surviving spouse has a high-paying job, if the deceased has lots of life insurance through work, if you have either paid off your home or have mortgage insurance, and if the family has substantial assets and few debts—your *additional* life insurance needs may not be significant. If, however, the death of your family's primary provider would result in a monthly income much less than the 60 to 70 percent goal, individually purchased life insurance is necessary.

If you prefer a simpler approach to calculating your life insurance needs, there is another rule of thumb for doing so:

- Carry life insurance equal to five times your annual income.

Though this formula is derided as simplistic by some expert observers, at least one such observer, NICO—the National Insurance Consumer Organization, a nonprofit public-interest organization—thinks the rule fairly sound. NICO says that the five-times-annual-income rule is applicable to most families with two young children who have group life insurance at work equal to at least one year's salary and who are eligible for Social Security survivor benefits. That's a total, then, of *six times* annual income, plus Social Security. So if you're the primary breadwinner, earn $35,000 a year, have one year's salary worth of insurance through work, and are eligible for Social Security, the NICO rule of thumb indicates that you need an additional life insurance policy of $175,000. NICO maintains that those with only one child, with a spouse enjoying a high-paying job, with substantial net worth and/or a good pension, or similiar benefits, can do with less insurance.

That 86 percent of American families are covered by life insurance sounds encouraging. However, of these people, the average amount of insurance owned was only about $60,000 in the mid-1980s. From this figure, the American Council of Life Insurance calculates average insurance protection for covered families equal to only 25 months of total disposable personal income. That's less than half what the rule of thumb suggests. In other words, most American families are underinsured.

There are undoubtedly many reasons for this. Key ones include lack of understanding of the importance of life insurance and what it should do; an unwillingness to plan ahead, especially about one's own death; and differing ideas about security and the future. And, of course, cost constraints prevent many people from buying adequate insurance. Unfortunately, it can be one thing to calculate how much life insurance you need and another to determine how much you can afford. However, there are ways you can cut the cost of life insurance. Two general rules are the most important:

- Buy the kind of insurance known as *annual renewable term.*
- Always *comparison-shop* for a policy.

Let's look at these rules more closely.

What Kind of Life Insurance Should You Buy?

There are hundreds of policies on the market, with a bewildering array of names designed to sound persuasive. However, all these policies basically boil down to two kinds of life insurance, *term* and *cash value* (the most common *cash value* is *"whole life"*). Understand the basics of these two kinds of insurance and how they differ, and you're well on your way to licking the problem.

Term insurance is the easier to understand. As the name implies, you buy this insurance for a specific period of time, a term. Its only purpose is to provide survivors with a cash settlement if the insured dies within the designated term. Its focus, then, is death benefits. There is no savings component or cash value to a term policy. You get nothing back out of it unless you die within the specified term. In this sense, term is "pure" insurance protection.

Typical coverage is for one- or five-year terms. When the term is up, so is your protection, unless you've bought a *renewable term policy.* With renewable term, you need not take a medical exam to extend your policy. You have the right to renew your coverage regardless of any changes in your health or occupation, until you reach the age specified in the policy, usually 65 or 70. Naturally, the premium you pay for this coverage increases each time you renew, to reflect the fact that you're older and so have an increased statistical probability of death.

Whole life insurance, as its name implies, is designed to provide *lifetime coverage.* Like term, it provides protection to beneficiaries if the insured dies, in the form of a cash settlement for the face value of the policy. But it also has a savings component, a cash value that builds up over the years as one pays premiums. The insurance company also pays interest on this cash buildup. If you give up your policy, you will receive this fund (provided you've paid into it long enough and your insurance company isn't "lending" you money to pay your annual premium, a scheme that cancels out much of your cash value buildup). That's why agents say, "You can always get something out of whole life."

It's important to understand that cash value is for the benefit of the insured, the owner of the policy, and *not* the policy's ultimate beneficiary.

If you should die, your beneficiary gets only the face value of the policy, not the face value plus the cash buildup. Although the insured cannot withdraw money from the savings component of a whole life policy (except, as just mentioned, by canceling or "surrendering" it for cash value, which eliminates the insurance protection), the insured can borrow up to 90 percent against it, usually at favorable interest rates. These loans can be used for any purpose and can be repaid at any time. Because of this cash value component, whole life is pushed by insurance agents as both insurance and investment.

There are many versions of whole life or cash value insurance. The most common is *straight life,* in which you pay the same premium each year of your life for the same level of insurance coverage; that is, the premium doesn't increase as you get older. The set premium is determined largely by your age at the time you take out the policy. There are also several sophisticated variations of cash value or whole life insurance you will be offered by life insurance agents today, including these:

Modified life. Premiums are relatively low in the early years but rise steeply later. This is a plan intended for people who want whole life protection but want to pay low premiums early on.

Adjustable life. Also designed with young families in mind. The policy is adjusted, in terms of both premiums and death benefits, according to need and ability to pay.

Variable life. With this whole life plan, cash values fluctuate according to the yields earned by a separate fund, which can be a stock, money market, or long-term bond fund. The death benefit also varies according to the performance of the selected investment fund, although there is a guaranteed minimum.

Universal life. A relatively new kind of insurance, but one that is currently growing fast, accounting for 38 percent of all new life insurance bought in the mid-1980s. Also a flexible-premium policy, it's designed to allow a policyholder to pay premiums at any time, in widely varying amounts, subject to certain minimums. The cash value buildup each year reflects interest earned on short-term investments. The amount of death benefit can also be changed fairly easily.

Universal life II (also called *flexible-premium variable life* or *universal variable life*). This policy combines characteristics of universal and variable life, flexible premiums with an investment choice. As with variable life, a separate account can be invested in various funds, with the cash value of the policy depending on the performance of the investment selected. Unlike variable life, however, there isn't necessarily a minimum death benefit.

Whole life policies offering insurance protection, cash value buildup, and premium flexibility—do these sound too good to be true? Is there a catch? Of course there is! And it's just what you think—the amount of the premiums charged.

To understand the difference between whole life and term insurance, let's consider straight life, the "granddaddy" of cash value whole life policies. Straight whole life works for the insurance company by charging a premium that is far higher in the earlier years than needed to pay death claims. This means that for a younger person, whole life is dramatically more expensive than term insurance—often five to ten times more! For example, a 32-year-old, nonsmoking male friend of ours found a policy costing $150 for $100,000 of annual renewable term (ART) insurance. For $100,000 whole life, he was quoted a price of $1500! He was being bullied by his agent nonetheless to go with whole life, so he asked our advice. We told him to look at it this way: A 32-year-old man has a 1 in 1000 chance of dying—yet with a whole life policy, he'd pay $15 for every $1000 of insurance coverage. That's a price 15 times as high as his risk of dying! This simply doesn't make sense, statistically or economically. He decided to go with term.

Of course, with ART, the premium for $100,000 coverage goes up every year, but only slowly for many years. By the time our 32-year-old friend is 45, he'll be paying about $370; at 55, around $800. That's against $1500 year in, year out for whole life. While it's true that at some age, the premiums would cross and term would become more expensive on an annual basis, that would only happen when the person was considerably older. By that time, his life insurance need might be much lower—or even nonexistent—because he would have retired, his children would have grown up and become financially independent, the mortgage will be paid off, and so on.

The advantage of ART insurance is that young to middle-aged families tend to need a lot of insurance protection at a time in their lives when it's most difficult to pay for. If you're one of these families, ART is the answer—

it provides the most protection at the least current cost. In fact, a key reason that most American families are underinsured is that they've been convinced to buy incredibly expensive whole life policies, so they don't feel they can afford any more insurance. But for the whole life premiums these people are paying, they could generally get five to six times more coverage by buying term insurance. Or they could double or triple their death benefits, decrease their premium payments from the whole life rate accordingly, and invest the difference at a good rate of return.

Arguments Life Insurance Agents Use in Favor of Whole Life

We want to discuss these arguments because it's guaranteed that you'll hear them sooner or later, and at first blush they will sound persuasive. Agents are trained by their companies to believe in whole life, particularly its "sophisticated" new variations. The first thing you should know is that whole life is far more profitable than term for the companies and therefore for the agents who sell it. It's not unusual for the agent's commission to be 50 to 100 percent of your first-year premium! Since (using the example cited earlier) 50 percent of $1500 is ten times more than 50 percent of $150, which kind of policy do you think the agent will push? To convince you to buy whole life, agents will use these five arguments:

1. *Term is temporary, while whole life is permanent.* In fact, term can and should be bought with a "conversion privilege" that allows you to convert to a whole life policy without a medical exam within a certain period, usually to age 60, if you want to. However, many, if not most, people don't need life insurance in their later years. After retirement, there's no need to insure against earnings loss. Social Security, pension, IRA, and other retirement income takes over, and these income sources don't stop with one spouse's death. Another thing: After 30 or 40 years of inflation, how much will a $100,000 "permanent" whole life policy really be worth? You'll have paid years of high premiums in relatively expensive *present dollars* for your beneficiaries to be paid off, years hence, in much less valuable future dollars.

2. *Term premiums go up every year.* True, but only gradually. If you buy term young, you'll enjoy years of low premiums and far higher protection than you could afford with whole life. And as you get older and your premiums get higher, chances are your income will have increased too, keeping you even in your ability to pay.

58

3. *Whole life is a way of forced savings; it's an investment.* True, to a small extent, but do you need to be forced to save? Even if you do, you surely have better vehicles—thrift plans, U.S. savings bonds, your IRA, and money market funds, to name just four. The tax advantages to interest earned on cash value buildup of a whole life policy (which are retained under the new tax law) are also available elsewhere. In any case, you have to be in a fairly high tax bracket for this to be very meaningful. As an investment, whole life is very poor. Most experts, including the Federal Trade Commission in a 1979 study, stress that the rate of return on whole life policies is inferior to what you could easily earn elsewhere. (Indeed, the FTC study concluded that rates of return on whole life policies averaged 1.3 percent. The insurance industry claimed 5.9 percent.) Note, too, that cash value usually builds up very slowly; you have to stick with the policy for years before it's worth much in that regard. For these reasons, you should never buy whole life unless you're reasonably certain of sticking with it for at least ten years. And yet studies show that one in five whole life buyers drops the policy within two years, often because it is so expensive! But dropping these policies so early makes them extraordinarily expensive, given the high premiums and little, if any, cash buildup. The larger point is, why think of life insurance as an investment at all? With it's hard sell on whole life, the life insurance industry has side-tracked people from the genuine purpose of life insurance—providing death benefits to dependents. Don't fall for the pitch to buy such low-yielding "investments." Instead, buy term insurance and invest your leftover disposable dollars. That way you get both more insurance and a better return on your money.

4. *Term insurance is money down the drain, whereas you can always get something back with whole life.* One variation on this is that "term is like renting your home; whole life is like buying." Another variation is that "you have to die to beat term," whereas you can make use during your life of a whole life policy. But term premiums, in fact, aren't wasted. They buy your family financial protection. And though it's true that you can get something back out of whole life, remember that cash values build up very slowly, and surrendering such a policy early can result in the worst of all worlds—no more insurance, high expenses, and little or no cash back. Also remember that when you die, the insurance company pays your survivors only the face value of the policy, not the face value plus your cash buildup. In other words, with most whole life policies, the company uses your cash buildup or savings to pay part of the claim! In a sense, then, your survivors are getting less pure

insurance protection, per se, with a cash value policy.

5. *You can do things with whole life you can't do with term.* Yes, you can borrow against the cash value of a whole life policy, once it builds up, and usually at good rates, too. There are however, often limits, or even disincentives, placed on your borrowing privileges and, if you do borrow, you're reducing your insurance protection until you pay the loan back. In the event of your death, your beneficiaries would get the face value of the policy minus the loan.

You'll hear these and more arguments for whole life over term. Don't fall for them! Agents will play on your love of family and will frequently provide misinformation. You might hear, for example, that whole life is "cheaper than term" or that it is "free over time" or "returns a profit"—all statements prohibited by insurance regulators in 36 states because they fail to take into account the *time value* of money.

Nor should you fall for the catchy new policies discussed earlier, like universal and variable life. Whole life has been criticized for years as a poor consumer purchase by NICO and other consumer advocates. So while agents will sometimes knock whole life and tout universal or variable life as breakthroughs in the industry, in fact, these new policies are only variations on whole life. Their advertised high rates of return are *gross rates*—that is, before commissions and expenses are taken out. Indeed, universal and variable life are frequently *worse buys* than standard whole life.

Now we know that the best insurance buy is annual renewable term, with a conversion privilege. With ART you get a bigger bang for your insurance buck.

Other Pitches to Avoid

There are a number of unscrupulous sellers of life insurance out there. Many of them are eager to prey on the concern that some of us have that we are "uninsurable," usually because of age. Beware the following promises and sales techniques:

1. *Guaranteed issue—no medical exam required.* This is the promise that "you can't be turned down, regardless of health." It sounds too good to be true, and it is. Guaranteed issue insurance is extremely expensive, because what it essentially means is that you're going to be charged as much for the insurance as someone who is terminally ill. That's right. The "no questions asked" policy is only a good deal for someone who would otherwise be rejected for coverage on medical grounds. In fact, it's not even correct to

assume that all legitimate life insurance companies or policies require a medical exam. With many companies (like USAA Life of San Antonio), if you're under 35, you can routinely qualify for up to $150,000 of insurance *without a physical,* unless answers to medical questions on your application raise a specific concern.

2. *Special group rates.* Yes, in many instances you can save up to 40 percent by buying term insurance through a group. But group rates are not always cheaper. Beware particularly of loosely defined groups, such as all people aged 20 to 60 or all veterans. For example, the group life program available to more than 2.4 million federal workers is more expensive than many available term policies for individuals! Not only are the rates sometimes high, but on occasion dividends on special group policies are payable not to you, the premium payer, but to the sponsoring organization. Also beware that what qualifies as a group may be changed by the insurance company. You may buy in with a group of ten only to find that in time your insurer's minimum size group becomes 100.

3. *"Graded death benefit."* Think about it. If a policy is guaranteed issue, why isn't the insurer flooded with deathbed applications? Well, the company may be, but it won't pay off much in claims. Why? Read the small print on a guaranteed issue policy. There's nearly always a clause saying that the policy pays a "graded death benefit." This means that benefits are severely restricted or even nonexistent for the first few years of coverage. For example, Academy Life of Pennsylvania offers a guaranteed issue plan for people aged 45 to 74. It includes additional benefits for accidental death from day one of coverage, but no benefits at all if death is not accidental! All the beneficiary of the policy would receive is a return of premium! Other guaranteed issue policies do a little better, paying a death benefit of 10 percent of face value if you die in the first year and maybe 25 percent in the second year. Because the death benefit is "graded," these policies are actually expensive for what you might get, yet they are nearly always touted as costing "only a few dollars more a month." Don't be fooled.

4. *A TV or mail-order pitch.* Insurance sold on TV and through the mail is usually hawked as especially cheap—"Only $6 a month" or "only $1 a week!" The catch? Your money is buying you very little coverage, often less than $5000. What's the point of so little insurance? If your concern is paying for a final illness and funeral, you'd be better off putting your money in a savings account. Another unrelated point about mail-order insurance is that most mail-order policies don't offer nonsmoker discounts, which are widely available elsewhere.

Are all mail-order policies bad buys? No. In theory—and *sometimes* in practice—buying insurance through the mail, thereby cutting out the commission earned by agent intermediaries, can save money. For example, USAA Life of San Antonio (which you'll be reading more about) sells *only* through the mail and is a genuinely low-cost source of life insurance. That said, it is still the case than many of the life insurance abuses just discussed are perpetrated through the mail. Mail-order life insurance is truly a case of buyer beware.

5. *Life insurance tied to student loans.* A growing number of insurance companies and agents are misleading people into thinking that they must buy life insurance policies in order to qualify for the government's Guaranteed Student Loan program. In fact, student loans insured and subsidized by the government are readily available through banks and thrifts. While insurers may legally offer student loans, it is illegal in most states to tie the loans to a life insurance purchase. So beware. You do *not* need to buy life insurance to qualify for a student loan!

So much for pitches you should avoid. Now let's get specific about comparison shopping for a policy.

Comparison Shopping

Once you've decided on the kind and amount of life insurance you need, start shopping for a policy. And make no mistake: despite insurance agents' claims to the contrary, comparable policies from various companies can differ dramatically in price—literally up to 100 percent or more! With many life insurance policies costing over time as much as a small house, the importance of comparison shopping for a policy can't be overemphasized. It can literally save tens of thousands of dollars over the years a policy is in effect. And the bigger the policy, the more important it is to comparison-shop. Yet, according to insurance industry trade groups, more than three out of four life insurance purchases are made without the consumer obtaining a policy comparison from a second agent!

Of course, cost comparisons can only be made between comparable life insurance plans. Compare ART to ART, whole life to whole life in the same face amounts. Here are some other features to compare:

- Whether the policy pays dividends
- Renewability and conversion privileges in term policies

- Loan rights, rates, and restrictions in whole life
- Grace periods before the coverage lapses

You must also understand that the cost of a life insurance policy is not the premium alone! Policies that pay dividends to you obviously reduce the policy's real or net cost to you. If you buy a whole life policy (which we obviously recommend against), the rate of return on the cash value buildup will also clearly affect its real cost. You must also consider what the policy will cost over a period of years. Don't be fooled by a policy with an unusually low first-year premium. Its rates may increase steeply after that initial "come-on" premium. Most of all, it is essential that the *time value of money* be considered.

The insurance industry unfortunately makes it extremely difficult to make accurate price comparisons between policies. Policy jargon about price is so arcane as to be unintelligible. So it's not difficult for one company to charge double what another does for the same coverage. Nor is it difficult to convince you to buy what are, in fact, outrageously expensive whole life policies over relatively economical term policies. Yet help for the consumer *does* exist. To cover all the various cost factors and to provide a uniform method of life insurance cost comparison, something called an *interest-adjusted net cost index* has been developed by the National Association of Insurance Commissioners, whose members are state insurance regulators. It's beyond the scope of this chapter to discuss how this index is calculated. Nonetheless, the index is the key to comparison shopping for life insurance because it's the only real way to compare prices between policies. The index takes into account the time value of money. It provides the most accurate measure of relative prices of comparable policies for given periods of time. Don't even consider buying a policy from an agent who won't provide you with its interest-adjusted index. Don't believe that the index is unimportant or unavailable or that all policies are priced about the same. Insist on knowing the index, with the understanding that the *lower* the index number, the less expensive the policy.

Remember, insurance companies will practically never offer you the index number on the policy you're considering. The industry, by and large, doesn't want you to compare prices. So you have to ask specifically for the index. Don't confuse it with a fancy computer printout "ledger statement," which companies routinely offer instead of the index. These printouts actually fail to tell you the real price of the policy because, again, they don't consider the time value of money. Even though 36 states prohibit an insurer from talking about the price of policies without factoring in the time value of money, nearly all agents do it anyway.

And for those of you who have decided that annual renewable term is the way to go, the National Insurance Consumer Organization has recently come up with another way to comparison-shop for policies. It recommends using the rates of USAA Life Insurance Company of San Antonio as a benchmark against which to compare any ART policy you're considering.* Although USAA Life rates are not necessarily the cheapest across the board (remember, a company may offer a bargain to a 35-year-old nonsmoker but still be high-priced for a 50-year-old), they are generally low. NICO advises that you look to meet or beat the current USAA rates (Table 3.1). You don't need to pay more!

So, for example, if you're a 45-year-old smoking man who wants $150,-000 worth of coverage, you'll pay $2.73 × 150 = $409.50 plus the $30 policy fee.

The table also shows the significant difference in rates available for non-smokers versus smokers, as well as *break points*—the levels of insurance coverage when rate discounts kick in. For example, you should be able to buy policies of $50,000 to $99,000 at one rate per $1000 of insurance coverage, policies of $100,000 to $249,000 for a lower rate per $1000, and so on. Break points differ by company and kind of policy, so ask the insurer how much you have to buy to get a discounted rate.

A final point about comparison shopping. The lowest-cost indexes in town won't help you if you buy from a life insurance company that's not financially stable. To be on the safe side, most insurance and consumer experts suggest that you buy only from a company that has an A+ or A rating, as awarded by Best's Insurance Reports. There are more than 200 such companies among the nation's 2000-plus insurance companies, so you'll have plenty to choose from. Ask the Best rating for each company your agent represents.

Sources of Low-Cost Life Insurance

First, if you are covered by a group life insurance program at work, find out if you can extend your coverage. The rates are sometimes as much as 40

*Taking the Bite Out of Insurance: How to Save Money on Life Insurance by James H. Hunt (National Insurance Consumer Organization, 1984).

Table 3.1 USAA Life Insurance Company of San Antonio Rates

Age	Man Nonsmoker	Man Smoker	Woman Nonsmoker	Woman Smoker
$25,000–$99,000 of Insurance				
25	$ 1.17	$ 1.37	$ 1.00	$ 1.35
30	1.21	1.45	1.00	1.43
35	1.33	1.81	1.06	1.68
40	1.85	2.61	1.47	2.12
45	2.73	4.00	2.14	3.10
50	3.83	5.72	2.81	4.68
55	5.71	9.20	4.30	7.31
60	9.76	13.74	6.40	11.17
65	15.82	25.33	11.19	16.49
$100,000–$249,000 of Insurance				
25	$ 0.98	$ 1.23	$ 0.98	$ 1.20
30	0.98	1.30	0.90	1.26
35	1.02	1.61	1.00	1.48
40	1.26	2.27	1.25	1.87
45	1.91	3.51	1.76	2.73
50	3.51	5.21	2.37	4.10
55	4.86	8.59	3.71	6.84
60	8.34	12.80	5.51	10.19
65	13.52	23.90	10.32	15.69

1986 annual rates per $1000 of ART coverage. Add $30 annual policy fee.

percent lower than what you can do as an individual—sometimes, but not always, so be sure to ask for the cost index numbers. One plus about extending your group coverage through the workplace is that premiums are usually paid by automatic payroll deductions, which many of us find less painful in terms of budget planning. However, a key drawback of trying to extend group coverage through work is that it is often not offered in amounts exceeding 2½ times annual salary, although there is no legal reason why that should be the case. If you follow the rough "five times annual income" rule, you probably won't be able to get enough coverage through a group plan at work. Another problem with group insurance through work is that if you leave the job, the insurance may be canceled or, if conversion to an individual policy is allowed, leap to a substantially higher rate. So know about the policy's conversion privilege if you elect to extend your regular employer-provided group insurance.

Another low-cost source of group life available to many of us is *veterans' insurance.* Although the maximum amount isn't very high, and the policy is frequently of the five-year nonrenewable term variety, it may be worth having, given its low cost.

In any case, group insurance accounts for only about one-fifth of total insurance premiums paid. That is, most of us are compelled to buy individual policies. So here are some places to look.

In New York, Connecticut, and Massachusetts, economical life insurance is available from mutual savings banks. The amount of *Savings Bank Life Insurance* (SBLI) has risen in recent years, and you may qualify even if you don't live in one of these states if a close relative does. Wisconsin also operates a state life insurance fund offering good prices.

Generally, the larger *mutual companies,* which pay dividends to policyholders rather than stockholders, are among the less expensive sources of life insurance. These include Equitable of New York, Phoenix Mutual Life Insurance Company, and New England Mutual. In addition, the National Insurance Consumer Organization, in its booklet "How to Save Money on Life Insurance," mentions several commercial companies in addition to USAA Life of San Antonio that offer generally lower rates. At the top of NICO's list is New York Life, a mutual company, whose policies are available through offices across the country. For younger people in particular, AMICA, in Providence, Rhode Island, is recommended. Connecticut Mutual, Bankers National, Transamerica Assurance (especially competitive for large policies), and Metropolitan also offer generally economical term rates, according to NICO. The GEICO Annuity and Insurance Company also offers low rates. For example, a 50-year-old nonsmoker would pay $380 for $100,000 ART from GEICO—$1 less than USAA Life. But at 60, that same person would pay GEICO $619, compared to $864 for USAA Life. So it's worth getting a quote from GEICO.

Other Ways to Keep Life Insurance Costs Down

Don't buy more life insurance than you need. This sounds odd, when we've noted earlier that the majority of Americans have less than half the life insurance they should. But there is a minority who has more than necessary. (One man we know, who earns about $75,000 a year, has a million-dollar policy, despite the fact that his wife has a high-paying job she intends to pursue for a lifetime and they have just one child.) An agent may try to convince you to buy enough insurance for your survivors to invest the proceeds and just live off the interest income. This is a poor idea. Few of us can afford that much insurance. But even if you can, it's better to buy a lesser amount and invest your "leftover" premium dollars elsewhere. Realistic and cost-effective life insurance planning should assume that the life insurance *principal* will be used by the policies' beneficiaries.

Be cautious about buying riders. They're usually expensive relative to the benefit provided. This includes the *accidental-death benefit rider* (often called double indemnity), which pays twice the face value of the policy if death is by accident. This rarely makes sense, when you consider that fewer than 6 percent of policyholders die by accident. Another way to look at it is to ask, are you suddenly worth more if you die in a car crash rather than of cancer? If you feel you need that extra coverage, what you're really saying is that you simply don't have enough life insurance. Another expensive rider is a *waiver of insurance premium* in the event of disability. (Instead of this, your priority should be adequate disability income insurance, which will be discussed in Chapter 4.) This rider generally costs a few hundred dollars and does nothing to provide the income you would need if disability should prevent you from working.

Should You Switch Policies?

Maybe you've been thinking you need more life insurance or a different kind of policy. And maybe this chapter has convinced you that you could benefit from some comparison shopping. Comparison shopping is always a good idea, but before you switch life insurance policies, consider these factors:

- If you've had a whole life policy for a long time, you may have built up valuable *loan rights* that you'd sacrifice in a switch. (With a recent whole life policy, the cash value buildup will probably not be such that your loan rights are very interesting.)
- Because you're older, any new policy you'd buy to replace an existing one would probably charge *higher premiums.*
- Many new policies come with a two-year *contestability period,* during which the insurer could decline to pay benefits for death caused by a preexisting ailment.
- *Dividends* on many policies have been increasing in recent years and may continue to do so, lowering your net cost of the insurance.

- Taking out a new policy means that you have to pay all those high front-end *acquisition charges*—mostly sales commissions—again.

For these reasons, as a bottom line, NICO advises that if you have an old dividend-paying policy, it's usually better to keep it and *supplement it* with ART if you need more insurance However, if you have term insurance and find that you can get it for a lower premium (compare index numbers and/or use the USAA Life benchmark rates), go ahead and switch, so long as the new policy has similar conversion and renewability provisions. Finally, if you decide to switch, make sure your new policy takes effect before the old one expires.

Some Final Notes

Life insurance proceeds paid to a beneficiary on the death of the insured individual remain tax-free under the new tax law. But a surviving spouse who takes the proceeds in annual installments rather than a single lump sum loses a tax break. Under the old law, that spouse received, tax free, the first $1000 of interest included in the annual payment. With the new law, that interest exclusion is eliminated for deaths that occurred after October 22, 1986.

Review your life insurance program periodically, especially when your financial condition or the needs of your family change. Remember that the proceeds of your policy will be distributed in accordance with the policy's provisions. Life insurance "passes outside the will," so its distribution isn't governed by the terms of your will (unless the policy is payable to the estate, which for tax purposes isn't generally advisable). So a revision of your will doesn't result in a revision of your life insurance distribution; the latter has to be done separately. (For more on wills, see Chapter 10.)

Keep your policy in a safe place accessible to beneficiaries—a place other than a safe-deposit box, which may be sealed by the court at your death. Give photocopies to beneficiaries and to your attorney. And if you move, be sure to inform your insurance company of your new address.

Summary

Life insurance is a complicated and technical subject at first encounter. Nevertheless, a review of key facts and guidelines will help trim the subject down to size and steer you toward the coverage you need for both your family's security and for your own peace of mind.

- Not everyone needs life insurance. If you have no dependents, you don't need life insurance. Life insurance policies on children are unnecessary. Homemaker insurance should be considered only after the primary breadwinner is adequately insured.
- The rough rule of thumb is that a primary breadwinner, with two young children, should have life insurance equal to six times annual income, plus Social Security benefits.
- For most of us, annual renewable term insurance is *far* the better consumer buy than whole life. You'll rarely hear that from a life insurance agent, however. So bone up on the material in this chapter so as better to resist the blandishments of sales agents.
- Other life insurance pitches to avoid include policies advertised as "guaranteed issue" with no medical exam required, policies offering "special group rates," and life insurance tied to student loans. Look out for policies with "graded death benefits."
- Always comparison-shop for a policy. Prices can vary by as much as 100 percent for the same coverage. Use the interest-adjusted net cost index to compare policy costs.
- USAA Life of San Antonio is generally a low-cost life insurance company. Use their rates on term insurance as provided in Table 3.1 as a benchmark for comparing other policy prices. Other generally low-cost companies are listed in the text.

4

Disability Income Insurance

FOR EVERY 1000 WORKERS BETWEEN THE AGES OF 20 AND 30, 789 WILL BE DISABLED FOR AT LEAST 90 DAYS BEFORE THEY REACH AGE 65.

NEARLY HALF OF ALL HOME FORECLOSURES IN THE UNITED STATES RESULT FROM MEDICAL DISABILITY OF THE HOMEOWNER.

Insurance is available to protect us from the financial consequences of disability. Unfortunately, only a minority of Americans carry this kind of coverage, leaving a major gap in our self-protection. But once again, safeguarding your financial future is just a few hours of planning away.

What Is Disability Income Insurance?

Disability income insurance provides you and your family with a monthly income if you become disabled and are unable to work for an extended period. Nearly everyone with an income to protect should have adequate disability insurance, but few of us do. Most of us are, financially speaking, better prepared for death than for disability. Yet if you look at it pragmatically, disability income protection is at least as important as life insurance. For one thing, adults between the ages of 35 and 65 have a far greater statistical chance of being unable to work for 90 days or more because of a disabling injury or illness than they do of dying. Moreover, if you're disabled, not only are your earnings lost, but you're actually a financial burden to your family. And for those of you without dependents, disability insurance is definitely more important than life insurance.

Sources of Disability Income Insurance

Most of us already have one or more kinds of disability insurance, but very few people can describe or understand just what they have. The most widely held disability insurance is through *Social Security*. Social Security pays more than $15 billion annually in disability benefits to more than 3 million covered workers and more than 2 million of their dependents. An individual's benefits are determined by salary and number of years covered under Social Security. However, the fact that most breadwinners qualify for these benefits shouldn't make them complacent, because Social Security disability alone is rarely adequate for an individual or a family to maintain an adequate standard of living.

To be eligible for Social Security disability benefits, you must have earned five years of Social Security coverage within the ten years before you were disabled, if you're 31 or older, less if you're younger. In other words, you don't have to be fully employed at the time of disability to qualify potentially. Nor do you have to be the primary breadwinner.

For Social Security purposes, you qualify as disabled if the injury or illness is severe enough to keep you from substantially gainful activity and if this disability is expected to last at least 12 months or to result in death eventually. The disability can be physical or mental. Many people don't realize that mental disorders qualify. In fact, schizophrenia is the third most common cause for which Social Security disability payments are made. Whether physical or mental, the disability must be "medically determinable." This essentially means that it must be certified by a physician and that you are under a doctor's regular care. It also means that you must be willing to accept rehabilitation.

The dollar amount of benefits for which you qualify can be calculated for you by a local Social Security office or an insurance agent. In addition, each of your dependents may get 50 percent of the benefits due you, subject to certain maximum levels. Under the new tax law, these Social Security benefits are tax-free if your adjusted gross income is less than $25,000. Moreover, once you've collected these benefits for two years, you also become eligible for Medicare benefits to help pay health care costs.

All this sounds encouraging, but the *top* monthly benefit for an individual is only $888; for a family, it is $1332—probably not enough to meet your needs. And the *average* Social Security payment to a disabled worker in 1986 was only $473 a month.

Workers' Compensation

The other commonly held source of disability protection is *workers' compensation.* Between 80 and 90 percent of the work force is covered under this program. It is the oldest form of social insurance in the United States, and disbursements are about equal to those under the Social Security disability program. All 50 states have a workers' compensation program, and the move in recent years has been to bring more and more workers under its umbrella. (Typically excluded from coverage are agricultural workers, domestic workers, the self-employed, workers in small firms, and workers in nonprofit organizations.) Benefit amounts are increasing, and compensation periods are lengthening. Many state programs pay for the entire duration of disability. However, state laws and rules on workers' compensation still do vary widely. So find out the rules for eligibility in your state, the proportion of lost wages or salary covered, and the duration of benefits. (Your employee relations office at work, your personal attorney, or any employment-related state agency can give you the information.) Also check to see if your state gives an extra allowance when the disabled worker has dependents. Altogether, your state law may provide for benefits up to 65 percent of previous take-home pay, subject to certain ceilings that would affect those of you with high salaries. You can also receive Social Security benefits along with workers' compensation, up to a maximum of 80 percent of your predisability monthly earnings. Disability benefits are usually coordinated, so that one program's payments are reduced in recognition of benefits from another program.

Workers' compensation has two big pluses:

- Coverage is paid entirely by the employer for the benefit of the employee.
- Disbursements usually start promptly, unlike Social Security.

Other disability protection programs that some of us enjoy are also provided by our employers. An employer may provide short-term wage continuation or disability income protection, a long-term protection program, or both. The short-term is by far the more common. Here are three key points about these employer-provided disability programs:

- Benefits usually start immediately.
- Benefits are usually substantial.
- Premiums are usually paid in full by the employer.

Benefits under short-term employer programs can run up to two years, although 26 weeks is the most common duration. Benefits usually start immediately, especially if the disability is due to an accident. Some policies may delay benefits one week if the disability is due to an illness. Nearly all short-term employer-provided disability plans pay benefits of at least half of predisability income; many pay two-thirds. Some plans will pay full salary for a stipulated number of weeks (sometimes determined by the employee's years of service), followed by a number of weeks at half salary. In most cases, employers offering this kind of insurance coverage pay all of its cost. In other instances, the employee is asked to share the cost. Less often, the employer doesn't pay for the coverage but arranges with an insurer for a relatively economical group plan for employees, who then pay for their own coverage through payroll deductions.

Employed mothers-to-be take note! If your employer provides this kind of disability benefit program, by law you must be granted a comparably paid pregnancy disability leave. Although you probably don't like thinking of pregnancy and childbirth as a disability, since the passage of the Pregnancy Disability Act in late 1978, that's what it is in the eyes of the law. This is not to say that a maternity leave must be a paid leave. If the company's benefit plan makes no provision for paid disability leave, it isn't required by law to make a special provision for paid maternity leave. However, if your employer grants paid sick leave in most situations, that policy must be applied to maternity disability, for the period of time a woman is medically certified as unable to perform her normal job functions.

If you're lucky, your employer may also provide *long-term disability income protection* through an employee group disability plan. Such coverage usually lasts at least five years and often continues to age 65 or 72 or even for life. Most long-term policies provide at least 60 percent of predisability income. As with the short-term plans, your employer may pay all or part of the premiums or may simply make group coverage available to you as an employee, with you paying the premium through payroll deduction. In some instances, disability income payments are included in profit-sharing plans or pension plans (the latter if the disability is "total and permanent"). Similar benefits to these may be available to members through their unions.

There are two other sources of disability insurance. First, if you're a veteran and your disability is service-related, you're entitled to compensation, no matter how high your income may be. If it's determined that you're 50 percent or more disabled, there's an additional allowance for dependents. These veterans' disability benefits are free of tax.

Second, some states (New York, California, New Jersey, Hawaii, Rhode Island) have cash sickness programs providing coverage for disabilities that are nonoccupational in origin. State disability coverage is short-term—less than a year—and the maximum weekly amount is usually less than $100.

To evaluate your existing disability coverage held through Social Security, workers' compensation, your employer, and so on, ask the following key questions:

- How many years of service are required for eligibility?
- How is disability defined?
- How are benefits calculated?
- What's the waiting period before benefits begin?
- What's the duration of benefits?
- Is disability caused by illness as well as by accident covered?

Although the disability income programs we've just described offer substantial protection, they are still frequently not enough for an individual or a family to live on comfortably. Don't forget that a person's disability brings with it many new expenses, frequently including household or nursing help. Or one spouse's disability may require the other to stay at home to provide care, thus eliminating the possibility of an outside income. For personal financial protection, most of us need to supplement these existing programs with private or individual disability income insurance. And for self-employed family breadwinners, outside the umbrella of most social disability programs, private insurance is a must.

How Much Disability Insurance Do You Need?

Anyone earning $12,000 or more a year is eligible to buy personal disability insurance. As with life insurance, the family priority should be to get adequate disability income insurance on the main breadwinner. Experts say that "adequate" disability insurance is an amount that will replace 70 to 80 percent of predisability income for low- to middle-income individuals and about 60 percent for high-income individuals. These percentages reflect tax savings, as the taxability of most disability benefits depends in part on your adjusted gross income—usually they are at least partially tax-free. Your preference is naturally to get as much of the coverage from Social Security and employer programs as possible, because these cost you little or nothing. So, using Table 4.1 or with the help of an insurance agent, calculate the benefits you would get from these programs and set that figure against your percent goal of your regular income.

Once the main breadwinner has adequate coverage, you can consider if a policy is needed by a secondary breadwinner or a homemaker—yes, a homemaker! Although there are no earnings to be replaced if a full-time homemaker becomes disabled, there is the cost of replacing the household services, and today, some insurance companies are ignoring the old $12,000 threshold rule, and writing disability insurance for these individuals. (It's relevant in this regard to note that, statistically, women are disabled more frequently than men. This is due in large part to maternity-related disabilities.)

Finally, you need to know that you can't just buy as much disability insurance as you want. Generally, you cannot buy private disability insurance that will pay you more than 60 to 70 percent of your current gross income. Insurance companies won't let you, on the assumption that when disabled, people who do better financially have little incentive to return to the workplace. For example, if you're earning $750 per week, you'll be eligible to buy private insurance of about $450 to $500 per week. Any Social Security or other benefits would be in addition.

To help illustrate the importance of adequate disability insurance and the need to approach it in a specific, practical way, let's look at the situation of one young couple. Robert, aged 26, and Marie have two children, aged 2 and 4. Robert is an office manager in a small company, earning $26,000 a year, and Marie works part-time in the local library. While driving home from a golf game one Saturday, Robert is involved in a car crash that leaves him totally disabled.

Robert's accident leaves the family badly exposed financially. He has not worked enough years to qualify for Social Security benefits. His accident was not occupational, so he gets no workers' compensation. His company does have a short-term disability income program that provides half pay for just 26 weeks, then quits. Out of the $1080 these disability benefits provide, Robert must pay not only mortgage, food, clothing, other household expenses, and taxes on the disability income (because his employer paid the premium), but also $175 for his life insurance, which, while he was working, was picked up by the company. Robert now also requires part-time nursing help costing $240 a month. Cutting out all but the bare necessities, the family can just squeak by, but only for the half year the benefits last. Marie is looking for full-time work but has little hope of earning what Robert did.

If Robert had examined his disability coverage carefully, he would have recognized its inadequacies. He could have made provisions to buy long-term coverage entitling him to $1600 a month for life through an optional group plan offered at work, for about $34 a month. The insurance coverage Robert needed to protect his family against financial disaster could have been his for a little analysis, a little planning, and a little money. It wouldn't have put the family on easy street, but it would have made the situation manageable. Instead, when Robert's short-term benefits run out, the family will have to seek federal Supplemental Security Income (SSI), a Social Security program designed to guarantee monthly income ($488 is the current maximum for a couple) for aged, blind, and disabled persons with very limited income and inadequate financial resources. And, of course, that won't give them anywhere near the money they need to live.

The worksheet in Table 4.1 shows you how to calculate how much private disability income insurance you may need.

How to Shop for Private Disability Income Insurance

The cost of private disability income insurance is determined by three factors:

- The dollar amount of income you seek to receive
- The length of the waiting time before benefits start
- The duration of these benefits

The latter two are really the key determinants because, as noted, the insured income amount is determined by your existing monthly income and calcula-

Table 4.1   Disability Income Insurance Worksheet

	Individual (single no dependents)	Family (husband, nonworking wife, 1 child)	Your Data
1. Gross income Annual individual wage or salary to be insured.	$30,000	$75,000	
2. Income to be replaced Multiply line 1 by 60% to 80%, depending on family need. In general, higher-income families need a smaller percentage of replacement income.	22,500 (30,000 × 75%)	48,750 (75,000 × 65%)	
3. Annual Social Security disability income Benefits depend on age and career earnings. Use 0 if your family doesn't want to depend on Social Security.	5,676	15,600	
4. Employer-provided disability income	0	0 (use 0 if your employer provides only a short-term program)	
5. Required income (subtotal) Add lines 3 and 4. Subtract total from line 2.	16,824	33,150	
6. Other income sources Add all annual earnings from bank accounts, money market funds, etc. Exclude IRA earnings.	840 (Assumes 7% return on $12,000 portfolio not in IRA)	2,660 (Assumes 7% return on $38,000 portfolio not in IRA)	
7. Disability insurance needs Subtract line 6 from line 5. This is the annual gap that should be filled by private disability insurance.	15,984	30,490	

tion of Social Security and other benefits in the event of disability. Obviously, the shorter the waiting period for benefits and the longer their duration, the more expensive the policy. You can choose a policy that starts from day one of disability or after a week, a month, or six months. If you're covered through work by an income protection disability insurance program that starts promptly or if you have significant assets you can draw down, you can better afford a longer waiting period to get lower premiums. Remember, too, that if you qualify, Social Security benefits will kick in at six months. If you have neither disability benefits at work nor substantial assets, you need a *shorter* waiting period.

Regarding duration of benefits, experts by and large advise to assume the worst—that you'll be permanently disabled and so will need long-term payment of benefits. How much good, for example, did it do the young father in our example to receive private benefits for 26 weeks when faced with a disability preventing him from providing for his family for the rest of his life? It's for this reason that NICO, among others, recommends buying a policy that covers you for life, or at least until age 65. To keep costs down, choose a policy that doesn't begin paying benefits for at least 90 to 180 days, if you can possibly manage.

What about some other ways to keep the cost down? Start by comparison shopping among several insurers for the best price for the amount, the waiting period, and the duration of benefits you've decided on. Again according to NICO, disability income policies are usually offered by high-quality companies at fairly competitive prices. Start with the major life insurance companies such as Equitable Life, Prudential, and other household names listed under "Insurance" in the Yellow Pages. Or start with the agent who sold you your life insurance policy, if you're satisfied you got a good deal there.

To give you an idea of cost, a 35-year-old man seeking $1000 of long-term monthly benefits, beginning 30 days after becoming disabled, will pay about a $600 a year premium. If he extends his waiting period to 90 days, his premium will drop to about $450. If an even longer waiting period of 180 days is selected, the premium drops substantially again.

Another key point when shopping for a policy is to understand its definition of disability. Some policies pay out only when you're completely disabled and precluded from *any* gainful employment. Other policies pay out if your disability keeps you from your *customary occupation*—and this is usually the smarter buy. Some policies will cover for *partial disability* (although usually only after a period of total disability); most will not. And some policies will pay only for disability resulting from an accident and not from an illness. You definitely want a policy that covers disability caused by both accident and illness, preferably for the same duration. Do *not* buy a policy that defines disability in part by saying it requires you to be completely confined to your home. Confinement is not a valid element of the medical definition of disability.

Next, make sure the contract is noncancelable, that it is *guaranteed renewable* so long as you continue to pay the premiums. Otherwise, a company may choose not to renew at the end of a year if your health should deteriorate.

Finally, don't rely on a *life insurance waiver-of-premium rider* as a substitute for a disability income policy. This rider provides that the company will keep a life insurance policy of a totally disabled person in force, without payment of premiums. But what comfort is there in a paid-up life insurance policy if there isn't enough cash to pay the rent?

Summary

Most of us are inadequately protected, financially speaking, for a disability that would prevent us from earning an income. We can remedy that by assessing the coverage we do already have and then supplementing that coverage as necessary. These are the key points to remember:

- The majority of us have one or more kinds of disability insurance in the form of Social Security, workers' compensation, employer plans, and veterans' benefits. However, there are a number of exclusions to such programs, and the amount they provide to those who do qualify is rarely enough to live on. So these plans must usually be supplemented by individually purchased coverage.
- With disability insurance, you should aim to replace between 60 and 80 percent of your predisability income. Use the worksheet in Table 4.1 to calculate how much disability income you would get from Social Security and other sources and how much of a gap you'd have to fill with an individual policy.
- To keep the cost of disability insurance down, take the longest waiting period before payments begin that you can manage—90 to 180 days, if possible.
- Buy a policy that will pay benefits for life, if possible. It should be guaranteed renewable and be valid whether the disability is caused by accident or illness.

5

Personal Safety

VIOLENCE IS AN EVER-INCREASING FACTOR IN HOME BURGLARIES. ACCORDING TO A RECENT JUSTICE DEPARTMENT SURVEY, ONE-THIRD OF THE ASSAULTS AND THREE-FIFTHS OF ALL RAPES OCCUR DURING BURGLARIES.

ACCORDING TO A RAPE HOTLINE CONSENSUS, ONE IN THREE WOMEN IN THE UNITED STATES WILL BE THE VICTIM OF A SEXUAL ASSAULT IN HER LIFETIME.

ABOUT 1.8 MILLION CHILDREN ARE REPORTED MISSING EACH YEAR—RUNAWAYS, PARENTAL ABDUCTEES, KIDNAP VICTIMS, AND HOMICIDES.

We Americans live in a world where personal danger is increasingly commonplace, but for some curious reason most of us seem almost to take violence for granted. We seem to do rather little to anticipate and avoid it, nor do many of us have action plans for dealing with it if and when it does arise.

What is it? Have we been so lulled by TV cop shows that we're "shock-proof," unable to distinguish between fictionalized and real dangers? Unfortunately, violent crime is increasing in the United States, but there are many things you can do to make it less likely that you or a family member will become a victim or, if you are a victim, to make it more likely you will survive.

Of course, personal safety is a subject that would take several volumes to cover in depth. What follows here, in capsule form, is intended rather to highlight the major problems and examine some of the more important safety habits that everyone should practice, especially those who live in or near major urban areas:

> First aid techniques like CPR and the Heimlich maneuver
> Street crime, and how to avoid it
> Personal safety tips for children
> The special vulnerabilities of the elderly
> Firearms and firearm substitutes—do they work or only make things worse?
> Guard dogs as pets—how effective are they as protection?
> Martial arts skills—how reliable are these self-defense techniques?
> Consumer protection and product safety—is your life being tampered with?
> Automobile safety—are our standards really adequate?
> Closing the loopholes in our "safety net," to ensure the safety of ourselves and our families?

Staying Out of Harm's Way

One of the problems we see again and again is the failure to anticipate trouble. What we need to do is exercise our "early warning devices" more often and see trouble in the making before it catches us off guard. But how do we go around expecting the unexpected? With a few relatively simple techniques we can train ourselves to be vigilant, ready for sudden action wherever we are—in our own homes, in the streets, in our neighborhoods. The closer to home the better. We need go no further afield than that to encounter potential dangers, and once we can cope with them on our own doorstep, we can do so more readily elsewhere as well.

First Aid Training

During the next 12 months, more than 650,000 Americans will die suddenly of a wide variety of causes, many of which are easily reversed if responded to promptly. For this purpose there are several skills that are easy to learn and that actually save lives every day. With a combination of these skills there's a good chance you would be able to save someone from death by drowning, suffocation, poisoning, choking, smoke inhalation, crib death, or cardiac arrest, because in many cases the victim's life can be saved by someone who spots the symptoms and performs the correct medical procedure in time.

The two most important of these lifesaving skills are *cardiopulmonary resuscitation* (CPR) and the *Heimlich maneuver.* CPR is an emergency first aid procedure used to substitute for or help restore the victim's heartbeat, breathing, or both. It is administered to (and only to) victims who are unconscious, have no detectable pulse and have stopped breathing. The Heimlich maneuver is used on victims choking (usually on food) while they are still conscious and able to stand. When the victim is no longer conscious, mouth-to-mouth techniques are used in conjunction with a variation on the basic maneuver in a prone position.

Here's how to proceed in a choking situation:

- Send for help, but don't wait for it to arrive.
- Ask the victim if he can talk. If he can't, he's probably choking.
- Strike the victim repeatedly between the shoulder blades with the heel of your hand.
- If this fails, use the Heimlich method: First, lock your arms around the victim's waist from behind. Then make a fist with one hand, back of the thumb against the abdomen between the navel and rib cage. Clasp the fist with your free hand and press in with a quick upward thrust—several times, if necessary.
- When the obstruction is out, administer mouth-to-mouth breathing if necessary and seek medical attention.

Like choking, cardiac arrest can happen anywhere, to anyone. A victim will have about four minutes before oxygen deprivation causes severe brain damage, and less than ten minutes before death occurs. If you act quickly and know what to do, that's time enough to administer potentially lifesaving assistance. CPR requires special training, which is usually available *free of charge* at your local Red Cross, YMCA/YWCA, or other civic centers. The American Heart Association has developed a four-hour CPR "Basic Life Support Course" taught by certified instructors. The instructors use life-sized mannequins that respond to the trainees' use of external heart massage and mouth-to-mouth resuscitation. Trainees learn the ABCs (airways, breathing, and circulation), three ways to remove a foreign object from a victim's airway, special techniques for reviving infants and small children, and the warning signals of a heart attack.

The important thing about first aid skills is that once you have them, not only do you have the ability to save someone's life, but also something inside you changes. With these skills, you feel more ready and able to face challenges that you might otherwise shrink from, challenges that call for sharpened overall safety and security-mindedness.

Safety on the Streets

One of the first exercises self-protection counselors teach is to be on the lookout not for "kinds of individuals" but for certain kinds of situations and actions. This is good advice for every member of the family, from the very young right up to the elderly. According to this rule, we should, for example, be on the lookout for an unfamiliar face that keeps turning up on the street, someone following you or taking photographs of children in a playground, or someone dropping a parcel or loose change or spilling coffee, creating a "minor accident" in a public place. These are events your early warning system should call attention to. Someone following you could be clocking your daily movements, the photographer could be using the camera to gain close access to children in the playground, and the "accident" could be a ploy to cover up pickpockets working the crowd.

An important exercise is to translate your vigilance into body language —actions and movements that telegraph your attitude, telling others around you that you have a purpose in mind, such as a specific destination and an action plan for getting there. People who shuffle along, daydreaming, counting cracks in the sidewalk also telegraph their attitude. Their body language identifies them as easy targets for a street criminal waiting for a "mark" to come along.

84

Next, a useful practice (especially for the young or the old) is to stake out territory around yourself as "your space" and don't let anyone near it. Make note, too, of the immediate surroundings, and be able to recognize any changes that occur in it, such as a bystander who suddenly disappears at the same time as a child or elderly person leaves a playground or parkbench.

Another precaution when setting off in the streets is to dress appropriately. Wear clothing and footwear you can move in, freely and quickly—flats or sneakers rather than high heels; no chains (which invite snatching and risk of choking) or flashy ornaments; purse straps across the body, not just off one shoulder; wallets or money clips in front pockets, not hip pockets (try putting a thick rubber band around the wallet, a nonskid device you'll feel if someone tries to lift it out). And don't walk home from shopping loaded down with parcels. Keep your arms free at all times, and your line of vision clear.

The following is a list of possible situations and practical rules of thumb for handling them. The need to draw on these tips may vary according to where you live, but from studying them you'll be able to recognize similar situations and know what to do about them if and when they do arise.

- Be aware that you're most vulnerable when you're upset or distracted. You're an obvious target when your mind is on other things.
- Vary your routes regularly when walking in the streets. Keep your movements unpredictable.
- Avoid taking shortcuts through secluded places—empty streets, public parks, alleyways, and parking lots.
- If followed, cross to the opposite side. If that fails, step off the curb and walk in the street where you can be easily seen.
- If the follower persists, call attention to yourself any way you can (blowing a whistle, calling out, even singing loudly) and head for the nearest safe place—any busy area such as a taxi stand or a shop.
- Take cover only in busy public places. Avoid empty vestibules, unattended elevators, vacant lobbies, stairwells, and other places where you could be easily cornered.
- When entering your own building, have your keys ready and out ahead of time rather than fumbling for them. When opening the door, stand facing sideways, at an angle to the door, to avoid being approached and pushed in from behind.

It's useful to remember that there are peak times of the day, week, and month when street criminals strike, usually coinciding with public paydays (middle or end of the month, Thursday or Friday). Moreover, robbers, purse snatchers, pickpockets, and muggers prefer to work under cover of poor light or darkness, so the bulk of their "hits" occur between dusk and 11 o'clock at night. Of course, there's no possible way to schedule all your movements around the criminal element, but if you live in a high-risk area and consistently find yourself on the street at "crime time," there are precautions you can take that will lessen your chances of being ripped off:

- Use the buddy system. Travel in pairs.
- Avoid late-night shopping or using automatic teller machines (ATMs) after hours.
- If possible, return home by cab. Have the driver wait for you until you are safely inside your home or building.
- Some people like to carry a second wallet containing a few dollars and fake ID cards to surrender if accosted.

Conforming your daily life with a safety routine isn't as foreboding it might appear in print. After using a given set of precautions a few times, "muscle memory" takes over, and you're on about your business as always, though much more safely.

Public Safety for Children

There's a classic magazine cover by a famous American illustrator titled "Not a Customer in Sight." It shows a barefoot kid in faded jeans waiting forlornly on an empty roadside beside a crude, hand-lettered sign: "Lemonade—5 cents a glass."

Perhaps this nostalgic image of yesterday's America provides a useful contrast to America today. Our roadsides are seldom safe for anybody alone, least of all kids peddling lemonade. Each year hundreds of thousands of children disappear from our streets and from our homes, giving rise to one of the most pressing crises of our times. While the exact figures are uncertain, one estimate is that 1.8 million children are missing in this country. Although many do eventually return home safely, thousands of others remain unaccounted for, victims of abuse, mistreatment, exploitation, and even homicide.

The first effort to deal with the problem at the national level came in

1982 when Congress passed the Missing Children Act. This was followed, in 1984, by the Missing Children Assistance Act. Later that same year, a special program called the National Center for Missing and Exploited Children was begun in cooperation with the Office of Juvenile Justice and Delinquency Prevention at the U.S. Department of Justice.

Today the center serves as a clearinghouse for information and assistance on issues of missing and criminally exploited children. The center conducts an outreach program to alert families, communities, lawmakers, and criminal justice organizations about the nature and extent of child victimization and provides training to law enforcement and child protection agencies to develop effective procedures to investigate and prosecute cases of missing and exploited children.

Although a large number of missing children are thought to be runaways or abductees by noncustodial parents, the fate of the majority remains uncertain. What is certain is that children who do leave home, even of their own volition, risk falling prey to the world of drugs, crime, sexual exploitation (child pornography and child prostitution), or even death at the hands of their exploiters.

To help prevent children from becoming missing, it's a good idea to have a set of official identity records made. Fingerprints and dental records are the methods most often used. Police usually provide fingerprinting as a community service, either at the local substation or, in some communities, in the home. Another method recently introduced is the *micro ID,* an information disk jointly developed by a dentist and an innovative policeman in Illinois. The disk, which is bonded to the child's tooth, contains the child's name, date of birth, address, and medical data and costs $15. Many dentists provide the bonding service free of charge.

Next, it's important to give the child, as early as possible, a set of guidelines to help the child spot potential dangers and to encourage the child to report freely any unpleasant experiences to the family. For this to work, it's essential to establish open and frank communication with children, to develop a "no secrets" vocabulary based on mutual trust and a strong family bond. The family vocabulary should include an agreed-on danger signal, a private watchword or phrase used only by family members in an emergency. Any time this word or phrase is used, a message is passed that only family members will understand and respond to.

Parents can instill and nurture this crucially important openness policy by listening carefully to children's fears and phobias, by being outspoken and teaching youngsters to be likewise, and by demonstrating to children that their instincts and feelings about other people can, and should, be trusted. Under this arrangement, a child who understands obedience can also grasp complex ideas to the contrary, for example, "It's OK to say no to any adult who does anything that makes you feel uncomfortable." The following are some safety rules that parents should start teaching as soon as a child can articulate a sentence. They are adapted, in part, from a pamphlet called "Child Protection" put out by the National Center.

- If you get separated from your parents in a public place, don't wander around looking for them. Instead, go to an information booth, ticket window, or lost-and-found office and report that you've lost your mom and dad.
- Never get in a car or go anywhere with another person unless you specifically ask your parents and they've told you it's OK.
- Don't go near a car that follows you or talk to the people inside.
- Grown-ups should not ask a child for help or directions. They should ask another grown-up.
- If someone tries to take you somewhere, yell as loud as you can, "This person is not my father (or mother)!" and get away quickly.
- Other people should not touch you at all, particularly on the parts of the body that are generally clothed and are considered "special" and "private."
- You have the right to say no to anyone who tries to take you somewhere or touches you or makes you feel uncomfortable in any way.

In addition to launching a child education effort, parents should also know what to do if a child does disappear. The following "runaway" guidelines, circulated by the National Center, are to be acted on by the parent promptly. The first 48 hours of a disappearance are crucial, although law enforcement agencies frequently delay immediate investigation on the off chance that the child will turn up voluntarily in this time period.

- Report the missing child to the child's friends, school, relatives, or anybody else who might be in touch with or hear from the child.
- Report the missing child to your local police and file a written report with the officer who responds to the call in your home.
- Keep a notebook and written record of all information on the inves-

tigation, including the officer's name, badge number, and police report number.

- Provide the police with a recent photo of the child.
- Ask the police to pass on the necessary information to the National Crime Information Center (NCIC) and to your state's clearinghouse for missing children. If the police won't enter your child into the NCIC computer, the FBI will. The 1982 Missing Children Act mandates them to do so, with no waiting period required.
- Make the child's fingerprints (taken previously) and dental records available to the police and the FBI.
- Call the national hotlines:

National Center for Missing and
    Exploited Children: 800/843-5678
National Runaway Switchboard   800/621-4000
Child Find   800/I-AM-LOST

You can leave a message at the switchboard for your child and ask that your child leave one for you. There are, moreover, more than 400 runaway shelters around the country. Contact those in your state and in adjoining states as well. They'll be glad to help and give you advice.

Parental abduction in many states is a felony. If your child is the victim of a parental abduction and the abductor attempts to avoid prosecution by fleeing to a state without such a law, apply to the local U.S. attorney for an "unlawful flight to avoid prosecution" (UFAP) warrant. If a federal warrant is issued, the FBI can then assist in the search for the missing child.

Fortunately, the chances of your child being abducted by a total stranger are very slim (fewer than 150 proven cases out of the 350,000 on file with the FBI), so let's turn from the worst-case scenario to some everyday safety precautions all families should practice:

- Children should learn to use the telephone (dial and push-button) at an early age. Regular exercises should include "telephone field days" when they can test their skills away from home.
- Preschoolers should know important phone numbers and addresses by heart. Memory skills can be improved by playing instant-recall games like remembering what someone is wearing after the person

leaves the room or license plate numbers on other cars when traveling on the road.

- Teach your child how and when to phone the emergency number, 911. (In 1986, a 5-year-old boy whose family had just recently moved excitedly dialed 911 and reported that his diabetic mother was unconscious and unable to be revived. The family's new address didn't appear on the 911 computer, but after conversing with the operator, he remembered the new address. Paramedics arrived in time, and the mother's life was saved.)

- Selective television viewing is another advisable practice. Television can have a potentially profound impact on young minds. (A 4-year-old Massachusetts boy recently saved the life of his little playmate, who was choking, by performing the Heimlich maneuver, which he had seen demonstrated on the comedy show *Benson*.)

Safety for the Elderly

Many of the safety tips discussed so far apply directly to seniors as well. However, as a group, the elderly are especially vulnerable in today's world and need singular consideration when it comes to personal protection.

One major security drawback for older people is reduced adaptability to change. The world of the elderly is often made up of little routines, things they've done a certain way for years. For the elderly, progress can seem just the opposite, as fixing something that's not broken in the first place. For them, little things can be the most disrupting: recorded messages instead of people answering telephones, changes in the way their bills come, getting in line and taking a number to buy a postage stamp at the post office, feeding a plastic card into an ATM to get some extra cash.

Changes such as these in the world around them, added to the internal changes that come with age (reduced sensory, memory, and motor faculties), adversely affect the older person's ability to cope with situations involving personal safety. Yet it's estimated that over 50 percent of all encounters with criminals could be avoided by taking minimum precautions. Here is some advice that we all, but especially the elderly, should benefit from:

- Don't go by appearances. Stereotypical criminals aren't the only ones to watch for. Muggers and con artists dress in pin-stripe suits and carrying attaché cases or Gucci purses just as bankers do.

- Never open your door to anyone you don't know, especially after hours. If, for example, someone wants to use the phone, direct them to the nearest pay phone.
- Be wary of ruses to disrupt your concentration—people asking directions, complimenting you on your "beautiful home," or creating a disturbance by staging an accident to draw you off guard.
- Take special notice of anyone who *insists* on helping you with your shopping cart, crossing the street, starting your car, or the like. (If someone offers, that's OK; if someone insists, watch out.)
- Never give out information about yourself over the phone. Don't feel that you have always to be courteous and polite, either. It's necessary to be blunt sometimes (tell unknown callers, regardless of the charity they're soliciting for or the product they're selling, that you'd rather hear from them by mail).
- If possible, have regular "pals," or belong to an organization or association that meets regularly to discuss security and safety topics. Share your experiences and your needs with them, especially the need to accompany one another in public.

Age and the restrictions that often come with it offer criminals greater opportunity, at reduced risk. For that reason, the elderly must take things in order and reduce their own risk factors one at a time. Seniors should carefully follow all the same guidelines people half their age do, but with greater attention to detail. Keep the pattern of your daily activities unpredictable. Vary your routine. Don't always walk the same route at the same time. The simplest precautions will work wonders to ward off juvenile pranksters, "Peeping Toms," prowlers, crank phone callers, even intruders; for example, outdoor lights on timers or photoelectric cells, a pet that barks at the slightest noise, a good noisemaker near the front door or near the telephone (either a "medical alert" or "panic button" linked to your security system or a "loud hailer" to call out through or even an aerosol-powered horn).

Some threats to the safety of seniors are not always so unwelcome. When the grandchildren are coming to visit, the elderly should take a few minutes to childproof the home. Put out of reach things that could cause harm: curtain cords over a small child's bed, electric garage door openers, power and gardening tools in an unlocked shed. When the grandchildren arrive, after all the hugs and kisses, lay down ground rules for the visit, rules that children will respond to when they're laid down with love. If certain rooms are off limits or if they shouldn't play outdoors unless you are with them, say so then and there. They'll understand it's because you care. After they've gone, once again check for hazards they might have left behind for you: toys on the stairs, food spills on the floor, furniture that's not where you normally keep it—anything that you could tangle your feet in now that you've got the house all to yourself again.

Personal Safety Aids and Other Precautions

The safety topics that follow deal with practices, devices, and products that figure increasingly in everyday life in America. Some of these we include as recommendations, others as questions we think should be raised in the interest of safety. Each of the topics may be more appropriate for some groups or modes of living or parts of the country than for others. As frequent victims of assault, women, for example, have safety needs that call for special consideration. Thus the following guidelines on self-defense methods are provided with assault victims especially in mind; however, each reader should ultimately adopt safety practices that he or she feel most comfortable in the long run.

Self-defense courses. Training in the martial arts is frequently associated with self-defense and is a course of action especially popular in and around major urban areas. Martial arts studies are good as disciplinary aids on several levels. First, they stress nonviolence over violence. On the physical level, they promote fitness, coordination, and precision, in preference to physical combat and brute force. On the psychological level, they stress mental and emotional preparedness, concentration, and anticipation of force by others. Disciplines such as aikido, judo, kung fu, and karate vary greatly in their style of first reserving, then releasing action in the form of avoidance tactics, or bodily contact in the form of kicks, chops, jabs, body thrusts, and tosses. Although each emphasizes different points, these studies all have in common the underlying principle of turning the attacker's force back on the attacker.

Martial arts have in common, as well, the years of study and practice it takes to master them. For that reason, we hesitate to recommend them as a first-line form of self-defense. Unless you are already an expert competitor, you have only a slim chance of getting off a chop to the throat or a kick to the solar plexus that will immobilize an adversary. Only a master of these skills would be advised to go up against a potentially armed habitual criminal who uses his skills to highly practical ends on a daily basis.

That said, in a crisis there are always uses for the physical and psychological skills that martial arts disciplines teach. The ability to stay calm in the face of danger, for example, can put you at an advantage over your adversary, who is nervous and excited. Your skills might open up opportunities that would otherwise remain closed, if, that is, you're planning to use a "hit and run" tactic. Just remember, however, that if you miss, you're back in the line of fire—your tactic can boomerang.

Instruction in the martial arts is available in most larger cities as well as in many smaller ones. Check the Yellow Pages under "Karate" or "Martial Arts Instruction." Some courses we've noticed are Alternatives to Fear (Seattle), Commission on Assault Against Women (Los Angeles), and D.C. Safety and Fitness Exchange (in conjunction with the Washington, D.C., rape crisis center). Costs vary; the average eight-week, two-hour-a-week course runs $35 to $60. Some centers, like the Chicago YMCA and the D.C. Self-defense and Karate Association, offer courses free of charge. For a listing of martial arts courses nationwide, contact the National Women's Martial Arts Federation, c/o Jay Spiro, 494 West Greendale, Detroit, MI 48203.

Commando tactics. Strong advocates of fighting back any way you can point out that certain commando hand tactics are easier to learn and require less specialized skills or physical strength than martial arts. We would caution, however, that what they do require is something even more demanding from you, namely, the intent to cause serious injury or even take a life.

Without going into gory detail, there are highly vulnerable pressure points on the body that, if gouged or forcefully depressed for just a few seconds, can cause shock or even death. These include the eyes (thumb pressure applied directly on the brain), a nerve center at the rear base of the ear, and the testicles. Going for any of these obviously entails first making close contact with your attacker. If you intend to call on the necessary instincts to stage such a counterattack (as when you feel your life is in immediate danger), we suggest first getting hands-on professional instruction, available either privately or, in larger cities, from special police divisions. Then rehearse the plan of attack time and time again with a friend. Don't wait until you're in trouble to gear up for something like this. You'll only get *one* shot at it, so if you plan to use one of these commando tactics, use it, don't mess around.

Firearms and firearm substitutes. The position of the national gun lobby is that handguns are generally the best of the self-protection devices, especially for the highly vulnerable. Handguns, accordingly, are said to be especially convenient for women because purses and handbags make for good storage and ready access in an emergency.

We take the opposite view. Most people who keep firearms for self-defense purposes tend to put too much faith in them. In actual fact, guns rarely help in a violent situation. For one thing, most home burglaries occur during the day when no one is there. And if you are at home, you could easily provide your intruder with a weapon to use against you, if he's not carrying one already. If he is armed, it's entirely possible the weapon is one stolen from a previous burglary victim. Firearms are the first thing burglars go for when cleaning out your closet or bedside drawer. The net result is that you're likely to wind up supplying arms to the very criminals you hoped to stop by keeping a firearm at home in the first place.

There's an even better argument against firearms in the home: Each year children in the hundreds are injured, many fatally, by guns that adults inadvertently supply them with. If you keep a firearm hidden somewhere in the house, you double a child's curiosity about firearms. Moreover, with gun makers advertising openly in magazines like *Boy's Life,* small wonder that guns keep turning up in the possession of 10-year-olds in classrooms at school and on playgrounds.

What about the argument that a loaded .38 automatic is good to keep in the closet "just in case"? Sure, weapons occasionally scare off a prowler, but so would a power siren and a yard full of floodlights all going off at the same time. Guns don't do the job nearly as safely. By arming yourself, you run risks other than being injured yourself. In some states, it's illegal to use deadly force to stop an intruder from walking through your bedroom in the middle of the night. If you're a burglar in New Jersey, for example, you can bring charges of assault with a deadly weapon against anyone, including your intended victim, for stopping you with a bullet. Even in Oklahoma and Colorado, popular "Make My Day" laws that allow property owners to shoot to kill are being questioned by the state legislatures after a number of highly publicized abuses by gun owners shooting unarmed intruders for trespassing.

Firearm substitutes generally belong in the hands of professionals, too. Aside from requiring, like firearms, the skill that comes from constant everyday use, weapons like Mace, tear gas, and stun guns are illegal in some states and subject to strict liability laws in others. Moreover, used improperly, they

94

often don't work. A change in wind direction can cause gases to harm the user. Stun guns require direct bodily contact with the assailant. Try touching someone with a powerful electrical current. If your attacker makes contact with you at the same time, you could, if not grounded, complete the electrical circuit and get the knockout surge as he does.

In sum, we feel that firearms and firearm substitutes are best left to the trained professional user who handles them on a daily basis. Ethical and moral considerations aside, nonprofessional users generally lack both the reflexes and the necessary intent to use lethal weapons properly. Few part-time gun handlers have intentions as automatic and as deadly as the weapons they carry. For that and other reasons, it's just as well if most people in their right mind really *aren't* prepared to shoot first and ask questions later.

Pets as safeguards. Many people keep guard dogs in preference to other forms of home security and personal safety. After all, a good guard dog is equipped with "sensors" that no electronic device can match. They can "smell trouble," come to the rescue if you're attacked, and possibly identify your attacker by scent at a later date. And you don't have to have a killer dog either. Any noisy mutt can fill at least part of the bill and, at the same time, make a nice companion for you and your family.

Of course, if your security needs are more serious, attack-trained animals are available from special breeders and trainers. Breeds most easily trained for this purpose are German shepherds, Dobermans, and certain strains of bulldogs. These animals not only make watchful sentries but can tear an intruder limb from limb on command—something to bear in mind if you are thinking along these lines.

Like certain security systems, guard dogs can be both incapacitated and unpredictable. We were recently at a social gathering where the host's two pets, a very alert German shepherd and a "semiretired" Doberman, were allowed to mingle with the guests. In the course of the evening one of us, first taking the precaution of introducing himself to the dogs, went out for a bit of fresh air in the garden. On returning to the party, the author was greeted, despite earlier precautions, by low growling noises. The shepherd, fangs bared, was blocking the entrance to the party. Without further warning, the dog lunged, leaving a nasty puncture beneath a ripped-away trouser leg.

As this story suggests, even "friendly" house pets can make very effective guard animals. Any dog, however, is only as discerning as its master. It's up to you, if you keep such an animal, to decide who the dog is, and is not, to mangle. These dogs need to be trained, and that's *your* responsibility. Don't leave to the dog a decision that's really up to you. While you're at it, make sure you carry liability insurance to cover any matters that do get out of hand. You can be sued not only for negligence but also for punitive damages if your dog has a history of biting. Such a history can also result in a court order to have the dog destroyed.

Your responsibility extends to the dog as well, and owning a dog can be a burden in many ways. Dogs often live to a ripe old age, long past the time when they can provide protection. The best advice in owning a guard dog is to make sure that you also enjoy the animal as a pet and a lifetime companion over and above your use for it as your household sentry.

Consumer Safety

Moving on from self-protection devices to a sampling of consumer items that call for a discerning eye brings us to *product safety*. Today more than ever, "forewarned is forearmed." The laws that govern the manufacture and sale of household products, medical devices, drugs, cosmetics, foods, and many other groups of products are intended to safeguard and protect users. Government agencies responsible for consumer protection in the United States include the U.S. Consumer Protection Safety Commission, the Food and Drug Administration, and the National Research Council. Government agencies, however, can't do the job without support from the public. It's up to the consumer to be informed, to make use of readily available information, and to take heed of test and research results that have a direct and sometimes critical bearing on personal welfare and safety. We will illustrate the point with two product groups, both of which involve life-and-death issues as regards their consumption and use by the public. Again, please bear in mind that the scope of the book is limited, intended to provide sample guidelines, not complete information on either subject.

Over-the-counter drugs is an area where consumer awareness is increasingly essential. This area is watched over primarily by the Food and Drug Administration (FDA). Each year 30 million Americans are victims of product-related injuries. Although a considerable number of these injuries can be traced to consumer carelessness, many others are built into the products and glossed over by skillful advertising and fancy packaging. But far worse than that, the number of fatalities from *drug tampering*—the intentional contamination of medicines with dangerous substances—points to another way in which personal safety is increasingly at risk. According to the United States Pharmacopeial Convention, Inc. (USP, an important drug safety standard-bearer in the private sector), the following are among steps you should take to avoid the risk of contamination, as unlikely as that risk might seem:

- Never take medicine in poor or insufficient light. Always read the label—every time.
- Take a few seconds to inspect the package, first before you buy, then again at home before using.
- Make sure the manufacturer's protective packaging feature (if it has one) is intact.
- Check to see if the lot number on the container is the same as that on the outer wrapper.
- Look closely to see if the bottle is overfilled or underfilled.
- Examine and compare all tablets. Make sure all have the same maker's imprint.
- Look for irregularities such as abrasions, cracks, or dents. Make sure capsules are uniform in size and color.

If you see anything you consider out of the ordinary about the medicine or its packaging, ask your pharmacist to look at it. If there are irregularities, your pharmacist will recognize them and, if serious enough, report them to the Drug Product Problem Reporting Program (DPPR). For emergency use only, keep a bottle of ipecac syrup in the medicine chest in case you are advised by a doctor or poison control center to induce vomiting.

Here are hotline numbers of important governmental agencies concerned with product safety:

Consumer Product Safety Commission	800/638-8326
Food and Drug Administration	301/443-3170
Environmental Protection Agency	202/755-0707

Consumer protection, product reliability, and user safety in the automotive industry are monitored by a large number of agencies, both private and public. As with other products where vital human interest is at stake, the standards of manufacture are a subject of constant review. Two official agencies responsible for scrutinizing the *car industry* and testing its products are the National Highway Traffic Safety Administration (NHTSA) and the U.S. Department of Transportation. They're the ones that, among other things, require us to "buckle up"!

Each year NHTSA makes public the results of dozens of road tests and catalogs manufacturing defects, mechanical problems, and related hazards on itemized makes and models. This information is for public consumption and should be used by anyone who owns or drives a car. In the private sector, several automobile publications, as well as Consumers Union, likewise road-test and publish performance evaluations on every car on the market, domestic and imported. Safety evaluations are an important part of these systematic reviews.

One important recent finding was that minivans are rapidly replacing the station wagon as the American family's car of choice. Sales for 1987 are expected to top 600,000, up from 40,000 just five years earlier. Many buyers of this popular vehicle are either unaware or unconcerned that the minivan isn't required to meet safety standards set for other passenger vehicles. As it turns out, the minivan may not be as safe as it probably should be for general family or other passenger-intensive use. The reason for the relaxed safety standards on the minivan, with its low-impact bumper construction and less-than-adequate rollover crash protection, is its classification as a "multipurpose passenger vehicle"—that is, both a passenger and a payload carrier. In this road classification, the minivan enjoys exemptions from the safety code not available to conventional passenger cars.

Anyone eager to own a minivan should first take a look at some up-to-date crash test results. Also get some figures from your insurance agent on premium costs. A top-of-the-line minivan with all the extras will set you back about $21,000, and cost $1000 or more a year to insure. For more information on auto safety standards, contact the National Highway Traffic Safety Administration. To report defective automotive products call the NHTSA hotline at 800/424-9393.

We will have more to say about car safety as it pertains to insurance in Chapter 7, but for now let's conclude our personal safety discussion with a quick update on *driving safety*. You don't hear enough about it, but there is a big difference between being able to drive a car and being a good driver. To qualify for a driver's license, you only have to know the rules of the road and be able to handle a car under nominal driving conditions. In other words, handling a car in an emergency is not a prerequisite for obtaining an operator's license in the United States.

From the standpoint of personal safety, being able to handle a car under problem-free conditions seems more like a starting point than a conclusion to driver training. Ask yourself: Could you recover a car that suddenly skids out of control? Do you know when it's safer *not* to use the brakes but to accelerate instead? Could you take the car off the road safely to avoid a potential collision? Very few drivers have ever experienced a controlled skid by countersteering into the direction of the car's skidding motion. The greater number, perhaps like you, are probably on the road because they scored 70 percent (or better) on a computerized multiple-choice exam and stopped at all the stop signs during the road test. Test machines in some states conclude the test when the score reaches 70 percent, exempting the applicant from even finishing! Does such a margin for error send the right signal to the novice driver? We think not. On the contrary, it implicitly sanctions a 30 percent margin for practical driver error, a tolerance that may squeak by under "normal" driving conditions but leaves many motorists underprotected when they most need a higher level of driver proficiency—in an emergency. We're told that the burgeoning number of cars on the road is the culprit and that the 55-mph speed limit is the solution. Be that as it may, our road safety record will always fall short of the mark as long as we educate our drivers to handle cars only under problem-free conditions.

The solution, instead of falling back on more governmental regulation, should instead come from individual drivers and interest groups like Mothers Against Drunk Driving (MADD) who take up the challenge to change existing conditions and to set higher standards for others to follow. Just as alcohol and driving don't mix, neither do armchair driving and road safety. It's essentially up to each of us to to gauge our safety needs, not by personal convenience or by law alone but by matching those needs to the degree of danger we face on our roads.

One way to go about taking up our safety slack is to enroll in a defensive driving course and learn, among other things, the specific steps involved in recovering an out-of-control vehicle. The more advanced courses allow you to experience the real thing under simulated conditions and to avoid a would-be accident in your path. The main reason, then, for taking a course in defensive driving is not just to reduce your car insurance premium 10 percent but instead to prepare yourself for hazardous circumstances, which today are anything but exceptional. A course in driving defensively will raise your sights and your confidence and qualify you as an "emergency driver," which is what your car can call on you to be at a moment's notice. The added protection that results from this increase in driving skill will make you, your family, and other motorists around you much safer on our nation's crowded streets and highways.

The following "good driver" tips, related to the fact that emergencies typically occur when vehicles are in motion, belong in every defensive driving handbook:

- Always use your seat belts! They restrict not your freedom but your *weightlessness* if and when your car goes out of control. You can perform emergency maneuvers effectively only if you're securely anchored behind the wheel and not floating helplessly above the controls.
- Avoid using equipment not related to driving, if possible, while the car is in motion. Dialing and talking on hand-held cellular telephones, for example, should be done when the car is stationary or by passengers only. All other activities not specifically related to car control should be kept to a minimum by the driver.
- Detached objects, such as briefcases, umbrellas, tissue boxes, road maps, food or drink containers, and toys, should not lie around in the car interior. In an emergency they become missiles—dangerous flying objects.
- Along with the other mechanical features essential to the safe operation of your car, the brakes, steering, shock absorbers and tires should be kept in top condition since they're what you will call on first in a moving emergency.

Summary

Awareness and concern for personal safety should enter into virtually everything we do, from climbing mountains to getting out of bed in the morning. Indeed, to write at length about all the various safety considerations of our everyday actions would take several volumes. We've instead chosen to single out the more serious things that can go wrong and suggest ways of both avoiding them and dealing with them if and when they arise. We hope that this information is useful to have on hand; we hope even more that you never have occasion to call on it. Instead, let these pages serve to quicken your senses, sharpen your outlook, and make you mindful of the vigil you must always keep. It's not really the mountain-moving task you might think. After setting your mind to it, keeping safe soon becomes as automatic as coming in out of the rain.

II

Property
Protection

- **INSURANCE**

- **SECURITY**

6

Homeowner's Insurance

FIRE WILL DAMAGE ONE OUT OF EVERY 150 HOMES IN THE UNITED STATES THIS YEAR.

A HOME IS BURGLARIZED IN THE UNITED STATES ABOUT EVERY TEN SECONDS. THAT ADDS UP TO ONE OUT OF EVERY TEN HOMES IN THE COURSE OF THE YEAR.

You can protect your home, personal property, and family against the financial consequences of fire, theft, and many other dangers. All you need is the right homeowner's insurance policy. But if you're like the majority of Americans, your home and belongings may be more than 50 percent underinsured.

The Homeowner's "Package"

Let's start by deciphering the basics of a homeowner's (HO) policy. It's not quite as complicated as it first looks. HO insurance is actually a "package deal," providing coverage on your home, unattached ("appurtenant") structures, personal property, and possessions. It also provides *additional living expenses* if you're unable to live in your home due to a covered loss. And

103

finally, it provides vitally important *personal liability* protection as well as payments for *medical services* for you, a family member, or even a pet may accidently injure on (and in some instances, even off) your property.

Here's an itemized breakdown of what a *standard homeowner's policy* covers and how that coverage works:

SECTION I	EXPLANATION
A. The Home	Coverage for the actual dwelling, including any attached structures (like a garage) and integral parts (heating, plumbing, electricity). *The dwelling must be used primarily as a private residence.*
B. Appurtenant Structures	Unattached structures on the property (toolshed, playhouse, detached garage, etc.), *so long as they are not used for commercial or business purposes.*
C. Unscheduled Personal Property	The home's contents—not an item-by-item list but broad categories (furniture, appliances, clothes, books, rugs, curtains, etc.). *Off-premises* personal possessions are insured for losses incurred in temporary residences (hotels, college dormitories, etc.).
D. Additional Living Expenses	This coverage pays living expenses in excess of what you would "normally" spend (on food, lodging, etc.) if your home is unlivable due to a covered loss.
SECTION II	
E. Personal Liability	Coverage that pays damages or legal costs if you or a member of your family accidently injures someone or damages someone's property.

104

F. Medical Expenses

Provides funds to pay for medical treatment for someone (other than family) accidently injured on your property and even for many injuries caused by a covered family member *off* the insured's premises.

The dollar amount of coverage you choose on your home (the actual dwelling) determines the dollar amount you get on appurtenant structures and personal belongings:

- Personal belongings are automatically insured for *50 percent* of your house (dwelling) coverage.
- Outbuildings are automatically insured for *10 percent* of that same coverage on your dwelling.
- Additional living expenses are covered for *10 to 20 percent*, depending on which of the basic HO options you select.
- Personal liability coverage is *not linked* to the dollar coverage on the house. All policies automatically give you $25,000.
- Medical payment coverage is automatically provided at $500 per person.

Neighbors of ours have a standard no-frills HO package with coverage like that just described. They've insured their home for $100,000 and so automatically have contents coverage of $50,000. Their large toolshed in the backyard is covered at $10,000. They have $10,000 additional living expenses coverage in case they have to move into a hotel in the event their home burns to the ground, plus the standard $25,000 in personal liability for use if their dog bites the little girl next door and, finally, $500 medical payments coverage.

You can, of course, increase coverage on your outbuildings, personal possessions, and personal liability by buying *supplemental coverage* for them. As we'll see, increased coverage on personal liability is necessary since $25,-000 of coverage is too little for virtually all of us. The insurance industry has recognized these inadequacies, and these standards are in the process of changing.

The good news, then, is that your HO policy provides a *broad range* of insurance coverage. The bad news is that within each category of coverage, there are numerous *dollar limitations, exclusions,* and *exemptions* that you must be aware of. You have to understand these to know where your vulnerabilities are and to determine whether you need to take out extra insurance protection.

We'll return to a detailed review of routine policy exclusions and limitations, but first let's look at the dangers, or "perils," as they're called in the insurance business, that your HO policy insures you against.

What HO Insurance Protects You From

There are six standard HO policy options:

HO-1: Basic Form
HO-2: Broad Form
HO-3: Special Form
HO-4: Renters' Form
HO-5: Comprehensive Form
HO-6: Condo Owners' Form

A key way in which these forms differ is in the number of perils covered. As you'd guess, an HO-1 policy is the minimum form, while HO-5 is the broadest. Table 6.1 shows how forms 1 through 6 stack up with regard to covered perils.

HO-3 is the most popular form, because most people tend to want the broadest coverage on their home and unattached structures but do not want to pay for such extensive coverage on their personal belongings. For those who do want extensive contents coverage, there's the more expensive HO-5 form. The HO-5 essentially covers all 17 listed perils, as well as any perils not specifically excluded in the policy. For this reason, it's often called "all-risk coverage." That, however, is a misnomer that can lull the unwary into a false sense of security, because *all* HO policies routinely exclude coverage for damage from floods, earthquakes, mud slides, war, and nuclear accidents. Flood and earthquake insurances are discussed later in this chapter under "Specialty Insurance," where you'll also find more detail on HO-4 (renters') and HO-6 (condo) insurance.

Additional living expense coverage varies by policy type. An HO-1 will

Table 6.1 Perils Covered by Standard Insurance Forms

Perils	HO-1	HO-2	HO-3	HO-4	HO-5	HO-6
1. Fire/lightning	✓·	✓·	✓·	·	✓·	·
2. Windstorm/hail	✓·	✓·	✓·	·	✓·	·
3. Explosion	✓·	✓·	✓·	·	✓·	·
4. Riots	✓·	✓·	✓·	·	✓·	·
5. Damage by aircraft	✓·	✓·	✓·	·	✓·	·
6. Damage by vehicles (not owned or operated by persons covered by the policy)	✓·	✓·	✓·	·	✓·	·
7. Damage by smoke	✓·	✓·	✓·	·	✓·	·
8. Vandalism	✓·	✓·	✓·	·	✓·	·
9. Theft	✓·	✓·	✓·	·	✓·	·
10. Glass breakage (where part of property)	✓·	✓·	✓·	·	✓·	·
11. Falling objects		✓·	✓·	·	✓·	·
12. Weight of ice, snow, sleet		✓·	✓·	·	✓·	·
13. Building collapse		✓·	✓·	·	✓·	·
14. Water/steam damage from pipes, heating a/c, home appliances		✓·	✓·	·	✓·	·
15. Damage from steam/hot water heating system		✓·	✓·	·	✓·	·
16. Damage from freezing of plumbing, heating, air conditioner, domestic appliances		✓·	✓·	·	✓·	·
17. Injury to electrical appliances, devices and wiring		✓·	✓·	·	✓·	·
18. All perils except flood, earthquake, war, nuclear accident, and others as specified in the policy.			✓		✓·	

✓ = Coverage for home, outbuildings; · = coverage for contents

cover such additional expenses up to 10 percent of the amount for which you insure your house. Policies HO-2 through HO-6 provide for coverage at 20 percent.

As noted earlier, all six basic policies provide the same personal liability and medical payment protections: $25,000 of personal liability coverage and $500 per person per incident in medical payments if you accidentally injure a person on—and in many cases off—your property.

Exclusions

Although your HO policy provides several kinds of insurance, there are many common exclusions you need to be aware of. Don't wait until you suffer a loss to learn that the following are generally excluded under the standard HO policy:

- *Commercial activities, if conducted in the home,* jeopardize your insurance coverage for the dwelling itself, its contents, and your liability to others. Even with just *part-time business activities* at home—piano lessons, child care, woodworking—you probably need an inexpensive commercial endorsement to ensure "total coverage." Discuss it with your agent, and don't try to fool anyone. (You may be lucky enough to have one of the new policies, which in 1986 included for the first time protection up to $2500 for business property kept on your private premises.)
- *Electronic equipment used regularly for business and kept at home* —a personal computer, fancy photographic equipment—is generally excluded from coverage (again, the new policies do provide some protection).
- *Merchandise for sale or delivery and samples* are excluded, along with business property you carry away from the home—for example, a portable PC, should you, say, leave it behind on a plane.
- *Cars, snowmobiles, motorcycles, minibikes, aircraft, and other motorized vehicles* are excluded unless (like lawn mowers or snowblowers) they pertain to service of the property and aren't intended for road use.
- *Rental property stored in the home*—party chairs, VCRs, carpet cleaners, etc.—all excluded.
- *Outdoor appliances and fittings*—including awnings, carpets, TV and radio antennas. Patio furniture is usually included.
- *Property belonging to roomers or boarders* unrelated to you is excluded.
- *Personal possessions lost from unlocked cars.* Coverage requires visible signs of forced entry into a completely locked vehicle.
- *Separately insured property* is not covered under a standard HO policy.
- *Outside help* (e.g., child caregiver, house cleaner, gardener) is gen-

erally not insured for on-the-job injuries. Most states require you to provide workers' compensation to such individuals if they don't already have the coverage or are not bonded.

- *Pets* (pedigreed or otherwise) are excluded. If your prize Abyssinian cat perishes in a fire, you'll not be reimbursed for the loss. (However, you are covered under the personal liability and medical payments sections if that cat accidently scratches a neighbor's child.)

- *Property under construction* is generally excluded. If you're building or renovating, you might not be reimbursed for losses (tools, uninstalled appliances, etc.) unless you are covered by special temporary construction insurance.

- *Property during household moves,* otherwise fully covered, is excluded while in transit.

- *Property kept at a temporary residence and lost during your absence from that residence.* This is a subtle one. Personal property that you, or a family member, take to another temporary residence is only insured from loss incurred while you are actually there in residence. For example, your son's room at college is broken into while he is visiting home at Christmas break. The stereo that is stolen is not insured, because he was not actually living at the dorm at the time of the theft.

- *Property in high-risk areas* (places like New York City and surrounding suburbs) can be excluded or limited to as little coverage as 10 percent of its declared value. (Special theft insurance for high-crime areas will be discussed later.)

- *Injury to others resulting from motorized vehicles* (aircraft, larger boats, other recreational vehicles) *used off the premises* is excluded —with the exception of golf carts, which are included!

- *Liability coverage for failure to render professional services* (adequately or otherwise) is disallowed under your HO policy.

- *Damage from floods or mud slides.* Unless you've purchased special flood insurance (to be discussed further), you're not insured if the creek or the street drain overflows into your living room. (You *are* covered from water damage that's "internally generated"—burst pipes, clogged washing machine drains, etc. And you are protected from wind and lightning damage during a storm.)

- *Earthquake damage,* too often thought of as a regional problem, can in fact happen anywhere and isn't covered with the standard policies. The special earthquake coverage you may want (to be discussed further) is inexpensive and widely available.

- *Nuclear radiation* is neither included under HO coverage nor available under other special insurance programs. Electric utilities, however, must subscribe to such special programs to cover their liability for an event such as what occurred at Three Mile Island.

- *Subsequent damage after an initial loss.* If you fail to take "reasonable steps" to protect your property from further damage following, say, a fire, any "secondary damage" from wind, rain, or theft is excluded under standard HO coverage. (However, if you do take steps to seal off and protect the area affected in the initial loss, subsequent damage *is* covered.)

- *Loss from power failure or heating or cooling systems,* unless that failure results from *physical damage* to those systems on your property. There's no coverage if, for example, a fallen power line disrupts power supply, resulting in the extensive spoilage of food in your freezer. (You could, however, file a claim with the utility company instead.)

Limitations

There are also many dollar limitations on the coverage provided by the standard homeowner policy. Learn these now to avoid some *very* unpleasant surprises later. The most significant—and startling—limitations are these:

- *A $100 limit under most policies on money, coins, gold, silver, bullion, and bank notes.* Yes, $100! Moreover, the $100 limit is in aggregate for the whole category. That is, you might be able to prove losses due to theft of $1000 in cash and an antique gold coin valued at $800, but the total reimbursement is still only $100. (An updated HO policy becoming increasingly available across the country increases that amount to $200.)

- *A $500 limit on securities, deeds, bills, debt instruments, letters of credit, passports, manuscripts, and stamps.* (In the new policy, the limit is increased to $1000, but still in aggregate for the whole category.)

- *A $500 limit, in aggregate, on stolen, lost, or damaged jewelry,*

110

watches, furs, and gems. Imagine collecting only $500 for both your mink coat and your diamond earrings! (The new policy will increase the limit to $1000.) You need a rider or personal property floater (to be discussed) to cover these items adequately.

- *A $1000 aggregate limit on silverware, silver plate, goldware, and pewterware losses* (increasing under the new policy to $2500).
- *A $1000 aggregate limit on loss of guns* (increasing to $2000 under the emerging standard).
- *A $500 limit on boats and other watercraft,* including motors, trailers, furnishings, etc. (increasing to $1000).
- *Limitations on camera equipment and advanced electronic gear* (PCs, satellite dishes, etc.). These limitations vary by policy, so discuss them with your insurance agent. (Remember, if it's equipment used for business, you are either not covered or, if you're lucky enough to have one of the new policies, it's covered to only $2500.)
- *On trees, shrubs, and plants* in your yard. You have only limited coverage if the loss or damage is caused by fire, lightning, explosion, vandalism, theft, vehicles not owned or operated by someone living on the premises, and (these next should be handy) riot, civil commotion, or fallen aircraft. Your protection is limited to *5 percent of the total amount of insurance on the dwelling*—for damage to *all* trees, shrubs, and plants—or no more than *$250 for any one tree or shrub.* That includes any expenses for removing and disposing of damaged trees. Moreover, your *landscaping is excluded* from coverage if the loss is from windstorm, sleet, ice, snow, or hail—the most common causes of such damage.
- *A $25,000 limit on personal liability*—as we'll continue to emphasize, that's far too little coverage in these days of drop-of-the-hat lawsuits. Even the emerging standard of $100,000 with the new policy is inadequate for most of us. You should extend your personal liability coverage under your HO policy to at least $300,000. This will boost your total HO premium by about $25. (If you have substantial assets to protect, consider supplementing the liability you carry under your HO and automobile insurance with an *umbrella policy* of $1 million or more. Its cost is small, about $100, and it could save you everything in the event of a major lawsuit.)
- *A limit of $500 per person per incident on medical expenses* for anyone injured on your property, regardless of who is to blame.

Off-premises accidents are generally covered if they result from your negligence (as when you tee off on hole 9 at the golf course and the ball hits someone on the head). This limit, along with others, increases to $1000 under the new standard.

Inclusions

After these long lists of dollar limitations and exclusions, you'll be pleased to read that there are a few unexpected items and situations that *are* covered by HO policies:

- *Personal belongings are usually covered against theft or other loss, even off the insured premises.* You should submit a claim if, for example, your suitcase is stolen from your hotel room. A good policy will also cover a suitcase stolen at the airport. There is usually, however, a dollar or percentage limit on off-premises belongings coverage—for example, up to 10 percent of the on-premises coverage. Jewelry, cash, furs, and other valuables are also covered off premises, but their special dollar limitations still apply. In addition, off-premises belongings coverage is excluded in some high-crime areas.
- Some homeowner's policies are written to include the *personal property that guests staying on the insured premises have with them.* In some instances this extends beyond the obvious. For example, if a dinner guest spills a glass of red wine and ruins her expensive silk dress, it's worth seeing if your homeowner's policy will cover it.
- *Damage to off-premises property by a child under age 13.* For example, if your 12-year-old accidently whacks a baseball through the neighbors' picture window or knowingly vandalizes their garage with paint, you should submit an HO claim. The point is that actions of a child under 13 are all treated like accidents, even if a weary parent knows better.
- *Accidental damage to someone else's property by you, members of your family, or your pet.* Personal liability coverage comes into play if the other party decides to sue you. For example, you shatter an expensive crystal vase in an antique shop, or your dog excavates a neighbor's azalea beds. File a claim; some companies will pay up

112

to $500 for incidents such as these, whether or not you were really at fault. Personal liability covers such accidents anywhere in the world.

Calculating Your HO Insurance Needs

To this point, we've discussed the different kinds of protection you get with a homeowner's policy—the "perils" the policy does and doesn't cover, common exclusions, limitations, and a few unexpected inclusions. We've also noted that more than half of all Americans are underinsuring their homes and personal holdings. So now let's examine how you calculate your homeowner's insurance needs.

The basic rule which you should go by is to *insure to value,* which you do in the following way:

- *Insure for replacement cost* rather than price paid or current market value.
- *Understand and adhere to the "80 percent clause" requirement* of the insurance company.
- *Review your coverage annually* and make any necessary adjustments.

Now let's see what these things mean. You start "insuring to value" by estimating what it would cost to rebuild and replace your home at current prices if it were completely destroyed. It's essential to understand that replacement cost is not equal to the original price paid for the house. It's pretty obvious that if you bought your house ten years ago, you couldn't replace it for that purchase price today, because construction costs have soared in the meantime.

Perhaps less obvious, replacement cost is *not* equal to current market value. After all, current market value of your home—what you could sell it for today—would include the value of the land it sits on, its infrastructure (foundation, incoming plumbing, electrical services), and appurtenant structures. So market value is usually greater than replacement cost. (A situation where this might not be true is if you have an old home filled with architectural detail that would be extremely expensive to replace, in which case the cost of replication might well exceed what you could get if you put the house up for sale.) The point is, don't mistake the amount of insurance you need on your home with the current market value of your property. If you do, you'll probably be overinsured, which is wasteful. Instead, with help from a professional appraiser, get an estimate of what it would cost at current prices to replace your house. A good insurance agent can often help you do this in part by providing you with a fill-in-the-blanks guide.

Next, the *80 percent rule.* Few homeowners realize that insurance companies require you to maintain your insurance at at least 80 percent of the full replacement cost of your home—or be badly penalized in the event of a partial loss. Only if you carry the required 80 percent coverage does the insurance company agree to replace or repair losses in full—that is, up to the dollar amount of your total coverage. (Obviously, you can never collect more than the face value of your policy.) If you don't carry coverage at at least 80 percent, you're going to be a double loser in the event of a loss. Here's how it works.

Say you're living in a $120,000 house (replacement cost, not price paid or market value). By the 80 percent rule, you've got to carry a minimum of $96,000 in insurance on that dwelling for the insurer to cover you in full for significant damage. If instead you carry, say, only $72,000 in insurance (three-quarters of what is required by the 80 percent rule), the company will pay only three-quarters of the loss you incur in most instances. So, for example, if you suffer a $20,000 loss, the company will reimburse only $15,000 of that. If you had met the 80 percent rule, however, by carrying $96,000 in coverage, the company would pay the full $20,000 loss. And naturally, if you were insured for the full $120,000 replacement value of the house, you'd also get reimbursed for the full loss.

By the way, the 80 percent rule does not apply if you have very small or very large loss. If, for example, the loss is less than $1000 and less than 5 percent of your total policy amount, you'll be reimbursed in full for that small loss, minus your deductible. Or if you have that $120,000 house with a $72,000 policy and the house is destroyed, you would get the face value of $72,000.

Table 6.2 will make the 80 percent concept easier to understand. The $15,000 at the lower right is the key figure. In this example, 60 percent of replacement value is three-quarters of what the insurance company requires for full reimbursement of a significant but partial loss—so you get three-quarters of the $20,000 loss, or $15,000. You have to make up the rest out of your own pocket because you've ignored the cardinal 80 percent rule.

If you find yourself in this unfortunate situation, there is one thing you

114

Table 6.2 How the 80 Percent Rule Works

Amount of Insurance You Buy	Percent Replacement Covered	Payment in Case of Loss Total Loss	$20,000 Loss
$120,000	100%	$120,000	$20,000
96,000	80	96,000	20,000
72,000	60	72,000	15,000

can check that might work to your advantage. An insurance company will sometimes pay, as an alternative to this proportionate reimbursement practice, the *actual cash value* of the part of your damaged or destroyed home. Actual cash value equals replacement cost minus depreciation. If the actual cash value of your partial loss (here $20,000) is greater than the $15,000 you qualify for under the 80 percent rule, you should be eligible for that higher amount. So check it out if you come out on the wrong side of the 80 percent rule.

The final part of "insuring to value" is to *keep your protection up to date*. Review your coverage annually to make sure it keeps pace with the 80 percent rule in the face of constantly increasing construction costs. (If you renovate or add to your home, you should talk to your agent promptly.) Despite the slowdown in inflation in the mid-1980s, it's a good guess that if you haven't upgraded your policy in the past five years, you're likely to be underinsured and exposed to potential serious loss.

In fact, many policies today deal with this problem automatically with an *inflation-guard endorsement*. This automatically increases your coverage quarterly or annually by a certain percentage. Some policies have *escalation clauses* specifically tied to local residential construction costs. Ask your agent about this low-cost extra protection.

Replacement-Cost Contents Endorsement

While we're still on the subject of replacement-cost coverage, let's extend it to the contents of your home. Unfortunately, only a minority of homeowners have replacement-cost coverage for their personal belongings. Indeed, in 1983, only about 15 percent of homeowner's policies included such an endorsement. The rest had the standard contents coverage of 50 percent of the insurance on the dwelling. And mind you, this standard coverage is only for cash value of the contents, or purchase price minus depreciation. Depreciated cash value is often only a fraction of what it costs to replace an item.

Most of us dramatically underestimate the value of the contents of our home or, more pointedly, what it would cost to replace today all the furniture, clothing, linens, tableware, appliances, art objects, books, rugs, and hundreds of odds and ends like pillows, pots, brushes, and brooms. To avoid discovering the hard way how much all these things add up to, you need a replacement-cost contents endorsement.

This endorsement is widely available at relatively low cost. Replacement-cost contents coverage at Aetna Life and Casualty, for example, adds only about 10 percent to your annual homeowner's premium. At State Farm, the figure is 10 to 15 percent. If you're a renter or condo owner, the extra protection for your belongings costs more—20 to 40 percent above the basic premium—but is still usually justified.

A few things must be understood regarding this extra protection: A replacement-cost contents endorsement is *not* the same thing as simply increasing the dollar amount of coverage you have on your belongings. That certainly is an option—you can pay extra and get contents coverage valued at 70 percent or more of dwelling coverage—but the problem of only cash value coverage remains. (Often when you buy a replacement endorsement, the insurer will automatically increase the total contents coverage to 70 percent of dwelling insurance anyway.)

Second, even *with* replacement-cost coverage, insurance companies usually pay only the depreciated cash value of the object lost *up front* when the losses are major. They make up the difference between that and the replacement value only later, when (and if) the item is replaced. This is because they feel that if they paid you full replacement value up front, you might just keep the cash and forgo replacing the item, which they see as cheating on the policy. So expect to have to go back and forth with the insurer before you get your full due.

There are also instances when replacement-cost contents coverage simply doesn't live up to its name. Usually, there is a 400 percent rule, whereby reimbursement for an item is limited to 400 percent of its actual cash value at the time of the loss. For example, reimbursement for an old chair valued at $50 when destroyed in a fire would be limited to $200 by the 400 percent rule, although it might well cost more to replace the chair with a comparable new one. Finally, policies usually won't fully protect items like oil paintings and antiques, for which a new replacement is generally considered impossible.

A replacement-cost contents endorsement does *not* require you to itemize all the contents of your home. Of course, there's the possibility that the insurer will contest the value of that $50 chair or even its existence. That's where the all-important and fully documented inventory (to be discussed shortly) comes in. For example, we recently suffered a loss that was satisfactorily handled due to our replacement-cost contents endorsement. We were loaded down with scuba equipment en route to Mexico on a dive holiday. While waiting in the boarding lounge for the flight to be called, we put our carry-on luggage down for a minute, and suddenly it was gone. When we got home we filed a claim, supported by documents that included an itemized police report and original receipts for the recently purchased equipment. The insurer promptly reimbursed the full replacement value (minus the deductible), based on the dive shop's replacement-cost estimate. Without the special endorsement, we would have instead received only the depreciated cash value of the gear and been out of pocket over $1000. This story also illustrates that personal possessions (even expensive sports equipment) are frequently covered off-premises.

Personal Articles Floater

What do you do to protect your special possessions, not just unique oil paintings but jewelry, furs, expensive camera equipment, and so on? The answer is a *personal articles floater.* This is available as either an endorsement to your existing policy or as a separate policy. The insurance "floats" with the specific articles protected, no matter where they are. (So if you travel a lot with your more costly possessions—camera gear, guns, jewelry, whatever—a floater is essential.) Coverage is also "all-risk"—that is, you're covered for any loss not specifically excluded by the policy. Floater coverage is generally individually itemized, with the valuation of the items supported by an appraisal and/or sales slip. Because value is established in advance with the insurer, you generally don't have the hassle of proving you owned a certain item or that it was worth thus and such when a loss occurs.

The cost for personal articles floaters depends on many variables. They are naturally more expensive in high-crime areas. Cost can also vary according to safety precautions you can prove you take with the protected items (expensive jewelry that's usually kept in a safe-deposit box, for example). Jewelry is perhaps the most common item for which a floater is purchased. Expect to pay $10 to $40 a year for every $1000 of jewelry coverage. (Yes, that's expensive. We know a number of people who literally feel they cannot afford to insure their jewelry. With jewelry that's been passed down through the family, it's not rare for people of even moderate income to have collections valued at $20,000 or more, which could easily cost $500 a year to insure.)

A final point: If costs for a floater and for an extra premium on your existing policy are about the same, it's probably better to go with a floater because it usually has no deductible and covers all risks. Note that once an item is "scheduled" (listed separately), it's automatically excluded from coverage under your regular policy. You can't collect twice.

Taking Stock

OK, so you've arrived at the replacement value of your home, insured it to a minimum 80 percent of that value, bought a replacement-cost endorsement on your personal belongings, and have perhaps added a personal articles floater. Now it's time to take a thorough and well-documented inventory in support of your policy. As time-consuming as it may be, this is an absolute must.

You'll see why you need an inventory if you pick any room in the house and, without going into it, try to list everything in that room—everything. Then go see how many things you've missed. When you think that a fire could destroy the contents of several rooms or even the entire house, it's virtually certain that without a complete inventory, you would not recover thousands of dollars owed you under your policy.

The inventory itself should be well organized, detailed, and as complete as possible. Your belongings should appear according to their customary location in the house, room by room. List the contents of each room in categories (furniture, clothes, collectibles, etc.). Describe each important item by any distinguishing features (model, serial number, maker's mark), date of purchase, price paid (with sales slip attached for major items), and an estimate of current value. Most insurers provide blank inventory worksheets, with spaces for itemization, but these are seldom adequate for anyone who has been accumulating things for any period of time. You're just as well off with a spiral notebook that can be added to over time.

118

Especially valuable items should be professionally appraised, and copies of the appraisals attached to your inventory. Moreover, the written inventory should be supplemented with photographs that clearly document the contents of each room, if not item by item, then from four different angles, with closet doors and drawers open for the camera. Two other ways to supplement a written inventory are with a video camera or your personal computer. The *video camera* is probably the easiest, most thorough, and least expensive way to do it. With the camera, go through the house room by room, and linger on (or zoom in on) special items or cluttered areas where viewing takes longer. Accompany the video with a written inventory or voice recording that logs the purchase date, price, and location of sales receipts. Special bargains can be had on one-day rentals of video equipment—as little as $35, with a deposit required. If you have a *personal computer*, special programs for home inventory are available, starting at about $20. The advantage of a computerized inventory is that it makes updating a snap, an important consideration since keeping your inventory current is essential.

After concluding your inventory, make sure you keep it in a safe place —a fireproof safe or a bank safe-deposit box—and file a copy with your insurance agent. This goes for your photo, video, and computer documentation as well.

Homeowner's Insurance and the New Tax Law

Under the new tax law, some losses can still be written off if a calamity occurs and your homeowner's insurance does not completely cover the damage. However, it is tougher than it used to be to qualify for a loss deduction and that makes it all the more important to have a good homeowner's policy.

The casualty deduction covers losses not reimbursed by insurance that result from theft, fire, vandalism, floods, hurricanes, tornadoes, storms and other natural disasters. However, the deduction is really limited to those who have suffered a truly major loss or a number of lesser calamities within the fiscal year. To calculate the deduction, first eliminate any insurance reimbursements paid. Then subtract $100 for each loss. Finally, reduce the total by 10 percent of your adjusted gross income.

Say you have a $20,000 loss by fire, 60 percent of which is reimbursable (meaning, you haven't followed the cardinal 80 percent rule!). That leaves $8000 unreimbursed and eligible for deduction. Subtract the $100 to get $7900. If your adjusted gross income is $50,000, you must reduce the $7900 by 10% of $50,000 or $5000. That leaves $2900 you could claim as a deduction on your actual $8000 loss.

This is actually the same formula used under the old tax law. However, it's less likely to come into play because under the new tax law your adjusted gross income will probably go up, since more income is subject to tax. Moreover, you're more likely to use the higher standard deduction instead of itemizing than you used to be—and if you don't itemize, you can't use the itemized deduction for theft and casualty losses. Finally, the real value of the deduction calculated above is lower under the new law, because tax rates are lower. All this tells you that you will not be able to rely on the federal government to the extent you did in the past to co-insure your losses. So private homeowner's insurance becomes more important than ever to protect your family from a calamity.

Comparison Shopping

Now let's talk about shopping for homeowner's insurance. Even if you already have a policy, it definitely pays to analyze it and periodically compare it to others. Some of the big names in homeowner's insurance are Allstate, State Farm, Nationwide, Aetna, Metropolitan, Liberty Mutual, and Kemper. The insurance section of the Yellow Pages is one of the longest in the telephone book. You might also ask friends if they have an agent they feel good about recommending. Spend a little extra time getting quotes from both independent agents (who offer policies from a number of companies) as well as from company-specific agents. Independents may or may not offer you a better buy, but they will do some of your comparison shopping for you.

The cost of homeowner's insurance depends to a significant degree on variables pretty much beyond your control. What insurers charge is based on their "loss experience"—what they've paid out in a claims area, adjusted over time. So if you live in a high-crime area, like a big city, you can expect to pay more than others who live in safer parts of the country. Your insurer also figures into the premium the efficiency and equipment of your local fire station, how far you are from a water source for firefighting, and what your house is made of. You'll generally pay a higher premium for a wooden house than for a more fire-resistent structure made of brick or stone.

The insurance industry is closely regulated, and state laws definitely affect (but do not set) the cost of policies. The existence of state insurance laws

120

does not mean that all companies must charge the same for the policies they offer. It may mean that in some states the more expensive insurers are required to notify the consumer that their rates exceed those required by the state. So rates do vary, and it does pay to comparison-shop.

The following points will help you save money on your homeowner's insurance premium:

- *Insure to 80 percent of replacement value,* not 100 percent. Remember that as long as you meet the 80 percent rule, you're completely covered for partial losses—and the great majority of homeowner losses are partial.
- *Increase your deductible.* All homeowner's policies have deductibles, generally around $250. While you have the option to purchase a $100 deductible, this will increase your premium about 10 percent and insure you more than you really need to be insured. Although one-third of all losses to homes and contents are less than $100, your policy should protect you against *major* losses, and you should "self-insure" against the small ones. So get quotes on policies with a $500 deductible, which should reduce your premium by about 20 percent.
- *See if you qualify for a new-home discount.* Statistics show that new homes generate fewer claims, so many companies offer up to 20 percent off at the outset, scaled down over a five- to nine-year period.
- *Smoke detectors, sprinkler systems, security systems, and certain police-certified precautions* can qualify you for a discount. Installing deadbolt locks, drilling and pinning sash windows, and reinforcing sliding patio doors (see Chapter 8), followed up by a certification inspection, can earn you a 5 percent discount in many states. A security system can save the homeowner from 2 to 12 percent, depending on the policy of the insurer and the degree of protection the system offers. Centrally monitored 24-hour-a-day systems are generally preferred by insurers over on-premises alarms (see Chapter 9).
- *Operation ID programs*—if you participate, you may also be qualified for a discount. Your Social Security or driver's license number etched on your TV, stereo, VCR, camera, and valuable possessions

helps police identify and recover stolen goods. Your police community relations office or public library will often loan out free etching equipment as a public service.

- *Are you retired?* If so you may qualify for a homeowner's discount. Statistics show that retirees spend more time at home, making their homes less vulnerable to theft and undetected fire.

How to File a Claim

If you suffer a loss, here's how to file a claim:

- *Notify your insurance agent immediately.* Most policies require this. Explain what happened and determine that it's a covered loss. Understand whether the deductible applies and whether the claim exceeds it. Ask how long it will take to process the claim. Find out if you'll have to provide estimates for repairs on the damages.
- *In the event of theft, notify the police immediately.* On filing a police report, you'll be given a case number. Note too the name of the officer, the precinct, and the address of the police station that will file the report. You'll need this to file an insurance claim.
- *Follow up promptly in writing.* Generally the agent will send you a claims form to complete. Return it as soon as possible.
- *Make temporary repairs to damaged property* to prevent further loss. Failing to do this risks invalidating your coverage for the damage. *Save all receipts for repair expenses* and submit them to your insurer for reimbursement. Likewise, if your house can't be lived in, save all temporary housing and related living expense receipts.
- *Expect a visit from an insurance adjuster* on larger claims. The adjuster will either be employed by or under contract to the insurer to verify the claim and calculate the amount of the loss. As a general rule the adjuster's calculation and the settlement by the insurer will both be commensurate with the loss you've suffered. However, if in doubt you might choose to bring in an independent adjuster who will reveal the *full extent* of the loss and negotiate on your behalf with your insurer. For example, if your kitchen is damaged by fire, an independent adjuster might include replacement of clothing, furniture, drapes and interior decoration damaged by smoke over and above the professional clean-up allowed by the insurance com-

pany. As a rule, you probably don't need an independent adjuster for a claim of less than $10,000. The adjuster's fee is usually 10 percent of the settlement, although some adjusters may charge an hourly rate of $25–30 plus overhead expenses. These overhead charges, which can range from $250 to $1000 on a $10,000 claim, ultimately depend on how quickly and easily the loss can be calculated, how much the insurance company complicates the adjuster's job and on how soon the adjuster is called in to calculate the loss (there's a saying in the business: "Cold ashes reveal less than warm ones")—so make sure an adjuster's services are needed before calling one in.

Note: you don't have to accept a settlement offer that you think unfair. Although most policies allow for settlement by arbitration, it very rarely comes to that. If it does, you pay for one arbiter, the insurer for another and you split the cost of a mutually selected third. But as with adjusters, the bulk of questioned or disputed claims handled by arbitrators is on commercial and not on homeowner losses.

- *Note that the insurer will initially pay only actual cash value* on a sizable claim, even if you have replacement-cost coverage. The difference between the two will be made up later, *after* repairs are completed or equivalent purchases are made. If you decide not to repair or replace, you get only cash value.
- *You generally have 180 days to complete repairs or replacement* and claim the difference between cash value and replacement cost.
- *Keep your claim active. Most policies have a statute of limitations,* so you can't just let it go for a while and pick it up later. If the statute of limitations runs out, you stand to collect nothing.

Specialty Insurance

Millions of Americans live in condos, rental apartments, and older homes. For these and other situations, specially tailored home insurance is available.

Tenants' insurance. As mentioned earlier, HO-4 is the standard tenants' or renters' policy. If you rent, you obviously aren't responsible for insuring the dwelling, but you would want to insure your own belongings. HO-4 covers your personal possessions against the same seventeen perils. HO-4 also covers improvements or alterations you make to your apartment at your own expense, up to 10 percent of the face value of your policy. Your personal property is also generally covered off-premises, except in certain high-crime areas. HO-4 has the same limitations on coverage for jewelry, cash, and other valuables as HO-3. The tenants' policy provides standard personal liability and medical payments coverage. Prices, of course, vary significantly around the country according to many variables, but to give you a rough idea of cost: in 1987 you could buy a $50,000 HO-4 policy with $250 deductible in Houston, Texas, for about $565. (If you rent out a house you own, it's still covered under your regular homeowner's policy for the usual perils. You are also protected against theft by your tenants.)

Condominium insurance. HO-6 is the condo policy. It's like the tenants' policy, because the condo association (like a landlord) is expected to carry coverage on the building itself. Structural changes or decorations you add to the condo are also covered up to $1000. As you calculate how large an HO-6 policy you need, check the condo association policy to see if it includes such things as appliances, kitchen cabinets, and other built-ins and also whether the coverage is for replacement cost. If it's not, unit owners could be asked, in a buildingwide loss situation, to make up the difference between depreciated cash value and current replacement value. So urge the association to expand its coverage to replacement value.

Older-home insurance. Some insurers offer a special policy to owners of older homes, because the replacement cost of such homes can exceed current market value. This is because the materials used, style of building, and architectural detail in such homes would be prohibitive to replace and in some cases also because old homes may be located in neighborhoods that have declined. The HO-8 policy allows you to protect your old home with impunity by insuring at the lower market value rather than replacement value. If your old house were substantially damaged, HO-8 would allow you to return it to serviceable, but not original, condition. In all other respects, HO-8 protects just like HO-3.

Flood insurance. As we've noted, your homeowner's policy does not cover for damage by floods or mud slides. However, if you live in a flood-prone area, low-cost protection is probably available to you through the Federal Insurance Administration. To qualify, your home must be in one of the 17,000 counties across the country that has agreed to develop and implement a land use control plan to diminish future flood damage. If available in your community, you can buy the coverage through your regular agent.

Single-family homes can be covered up to $185,000, with contents covered at a maximum of $60,000. With the standard $500 deductible, the premium on an $85,000 home (contents not included) is about $165 a year. The federal government provides a toll-free number (800/638-6620) to answer any questions you might have.

Crime insurance. The Federal Crime Insurance Program is designed to fill the gap left by private insurers who refuse to provide coverage for theft in high-crime areas. The government determines which areas have access to this program. It's currently available in parts of nearly 30 states. New York alone, however, accounts for nearly two-thirds of all federal crime insurance policies written. The maximum protection offered, however, only is $10,000, with a deductible of $100 or 5 percent of the gross loss, whichever is greater. Not only is the maximum coverage low, but the other bad news is that the really "hot" items for the urban burglar—guns, jewelry, cash, furs, cameras —are limited to $500 coverage a hit. In addition, the government stipulates that you have certain door and window locks in order to qualify. Crime insurance costs $60 for $1000 of coverage and $120 for $10,000—the latter clearly the better buy. If available in your community, you can buy it from your regular insurance agent. For further information, you can call the federal insurer's office at 800/638-8780.

Mortgage insurance. This is a term life insurance policy, linked to your mortgage payment, which pays off the mortgage if you die or become disabled. Some people buy this protection only against untimely death. That's a mistake. If you've determined that you need mortgage insurance, you should pay extra to get it for disability as well. (It's not, however, a substitute for disability income insurance.) You buy mortgage insurance in the amount of your mortgage (often through your mortgage company), and like the mortgage, it declines over time. Premiums are set according to your age at the time of purchase. Payments are generally made through the lender as part of your monthly payment. They are constant over time despite the fact that the mortgage, and so the real value to you of the policy, is decreasing. This tells you that mortgage insurance is a better deal when your mortgage balance is high but becomes less valuable as the years pass.

You should consider mortgage insurance if the death or disability of either member of a working couple would leave the remaining person really strapped to meet monthly payments. The alternative, of course, is simply to increase your term life insurance. Proceeds from the life insurance can be used to pay off or pay down the mortgage or could be invested in liquid assets (such as money market funds) and used to meet the monthly payment. Increasing your term life insurance may ultimately be smarter than buying mortgage insurance because paying off the mortgage via mortgage insurance eliminates one of the few remaining tax write-offs under the 1986 tax reform legislation.

Here is a poignant story: Our insurance agent told us of a 40-year-old man with three children who, after owning his expensive home for a few years, suddenly decided to take out insurance on his remaining mortgage balance. Three weeks after doing so, he dropped dead of a heart attack. The agent said he never felt better about delivering a check.

Mortgage insurance is, of course, available for either or both spouses, with joint coverage paying off if either dies or is disabled. As with most insurance policies, prices vary significantly according to your particular circumstances. As a rough example, a nonsmoking man aged 35 with an $85,000 mortgage would pay about $215 for coverage. To extend coverage to his 35-year-old wife would cost an added $180. The comparable figures for smokers are $370 and $325.

Summary

Homeowner's insurance is one of the most vital forms of protection you can buy. Inadequate coverage can leave you and your family disastrously vulnerable. Here are ten key points on HO coverage:

- Insure to a minimum 80 percent of replacement value.
- Buy a replacement-cost endorsement on the contents of your home.
- Know your policy's exclusions and dollar limitations. Plan for extra protection accordingly. A personal articles floater is the best way to protect special valuables.
- Extend your personal liability coverage to a minimum of $300,000. If you have substantial assets, buy an umbrella policy of a million dollars or more.
- Keep an updated, detailed inventory of your belongings, supported with receipts, photographs, and/or video recordings. Store the originals in a safe place, and send a duplicate set to your insurer.
- Notify your agent immediately when a loss occurs. Make any tem-

porary repairs necessary to forestall further damage, and save all receipts.

- When in doubt, file a claim. A lot of odd instances are in fact covered, so it always pays to file.
- Your homeowner's policy is an evolving document requiring at least annual review. Purchase an inflation guard endorsement to keep current with local market conditions.
- To save on your insurance premium, always comparison-shop, insure to 80 percent versus 100 percent of value, increase your deductibles, and aggressively seek out discounts for such things as retirement status and security systems.
- Watch for an innovative product line that recognizes insurance as a form of security and vice versa. A major insurer recently joined forces with a prestigious home security company to offer an insurance/security package that could prove a good consumer deal. For details on this new dual-protection product see Chapter 9.

7

Automobile Insurance and Car Security Systems

MOST PEOPLE BUY THE CAR INSURANCE THEY'RE PERSUADED TO BUY, NOT THE COVERAGE THEY REALLY NEED.

MANY PEOPLE ARE DANGEROUSLY UNDERINSURED FOR LIABILITY (CURRENTLY REQUIRED BY LAW IN ABOUT HALF THE STATES) COMPARED TO WHAT THEY STAND TO LOSE IN THE EVENT OF A LEGAL JUDGMENT AGAINST THEM.

AN ANTITHEFT DEVICE ON YOUR CAR CAN QUALIFY YOU FOR A SUBSTANTIAL INSURANCE DISCOUNT.

The kind of automobile insurance coverage you carry, and the annual premium you pay for it, involves making some pretty informed choices. Understanding how car insurance works and how policies are written will point you toward the kind coverage you need at rates competitive with, or even below,

129

the current average in today's market. Without understanding car insurance basics, you risk buying either a fully loaded, low-deductible policy that can cost as much as double what you need pay for adequate coverage, or too little insurance (or the wrong kind), which will leave you inadequately protected. The secret is knowing what your choices are to start with and recognizing the warning signs of things to be avoided.

To simplify the car insurance selection process, let's start by eliminating factors you have no direct control over. First off, insurance costs vary substantially according to where you live—not just from state to state but even from city to city or area to area within a city. This is because of local laws and local risks. If the law and local risk in your state double the cost of your insurance (identical coverage can vary from state to state by as much as 100 precent), about the only thing you can do is register your car in another state—not very practical (and not very legal, either).

Likewise, how insurance companies arrive at and interpret statistics that determine rating guidelines and set claims limits, exclusions, and "loss experiences" are also factors we have little control over. Our state insurance boards are there to do that for us, to watch over the collection and interpretation of data and to make sure that the standards they set are met by the insurance industry. Nor have we any control over the safety factors that ultimately determine the amount of coverage we need and what that coverage will cost us—for example, the fact that drivers under 25 are involved in over 35 percent of accidents reported, which drives up the cost of insurance for us all.

Still, as informed consumers, there is lot we can do to make sure we get the best car insurance for the least amount of money. The average car insurance premium has recently risen to over $550 a year, but you can save as much as 50 percent by comparison shopping and buying only what you need. Remember, expensive or excessive insurance isn't the same thing as total coverage. Yet car insurance shoppers still often buy what they're persuaded to buy and not what they need. There are a lot of insurance agents around who push the "standard policy," loaded with all the trimmings, on unsuspecting customers who then wind up overinsured on the more expensive collision and comprehensive policies and underinsured on the less expensive (but more important) liability coverages. More on that in a minute, after we've explained what these different coverages are. Let's just say that by having a clear picture of how the car insurance industry works, informed shoppers can avoid this kind of imbalanced coverage. So let's start by

130

breaking automobile insurance down into its basic parts and examining each in turn.

Car Insurance Coverages

There are, in all, seven different types of coverage available in every standard automobile policy—four basic coverages and three supplementary coverages. These coverages are either mandatory or optional and vary from one state to another:

BASIC

Bodily injury liability	*(usually mandatory)*
Property damage liability	*(usually mandatory)*
Comprehensive	*(optional)*
Collision	*(optional)*

SUPPLEMENTARY

"No fault"	*(varies by state)*
Medical payments	*(optional)*
Uninsured motorists	*(optional)*

Four Basic Coverages

Liability coverage, made up of bodily injury and property damage, protects others against the consequences of accidents caused by you, the policyholder. In states where liability coverage is required by law (currently about half the states have a minimum requirement), documents showing proof of insurance must be carried in the vehicle at all times. Any driver stopped without insurance documents can expect a heavy fine if unable to show proof of insurance in court. Furthermore, anyone involved in an accident without the required minimum of liability coverage may be required to purchase, in addition to the hefty fine, special "high-risk" (and so, high-cost) insurance or even have his or her driver's license revoked completely.

Liability insurance breaks down in the following way:

Bodily injury liability covers the consequences of an accident in which others are injured or killed by your car (other drivers and their passengers, pedestrians, guests in your car, and another driver of your car, so long as that driver has your consent). You are also covered while driving someone else's car with the owner's permission. This coverage provides protection in the form of legal defense and, in the event that you are held legally liable for injuries caused, payment of damages assessed against you up to the limits stated in the policy.

Property damage liability covers damage to the property of others in much the same way that bodily injury coverage does. It insures any property that you, or anyone driving your car with your permission, might damage, including other cars, buildings, lampposts, and telephone poles. You and your family members are also covered while driving someone else's car with their permission. In the event of a claim or lawsuit against you, this coverage provides protection in the form of legal defense and payment for any damages for which you are legally liable, up to the limits of the policy.

In states where liability insurance is mandatory, there's a *minimum coverage requirement.* Starting with the legal minimum, the limits of liability coverage are set at the time of purchase by the buyer according to need. Personal injury and property damage limits are always stated together in a three-unit grouping. The minimum requirement in states that have a liability law is typically something like 25/50/10—the first number refers to the limit payable on any one person, the second is the maximum payable on any one accident, and the third is the maximum on property damage, all stated in thousands of dollars. According to consumer groups, however, the required minimum is below what is necessary. The average driver, according to their advice, should carry liability coverage of 100/300/50—that is, the policy should pay up to $100,000 for a single injury, but no more than $300,000 for all injuries in any one accident, and up to $50,000 in property damage. The question is, how much liability coverage do *you* need? Are you an "average" or better-than-average driver, and are your protection needs greater than what the minimum requirement covers you for? Since the choice is yours (and it's an important one), we'll come back to this later.

So much for the two basic insurance coverages generally required by law and there to protect others against you. Another coverage that is becoming increasingly popular and is already mandatory in some states is "No fault" insurance, and we'll get to that in a minute. First, let's look at the other two remaining basic coverages listed, both of which are optional and are intended to protect your car against either "acts of nature" or "acts of others."

Comprehensive physical damage protects your motor vehicle against everything except collision with another car or object. Under this coverage, your car is insured against theft, vandalism, fire, glass breakage and falling objects caused by missiles, explosions, civil riots, and natural calamities such as earthquakes, floods, windstorms, or hail.

Collision insurance, the last of the four basic coverages, pays damages to your car as well, but this time as the result of colliding with another car or object or overturning. Under collision coverage, payment is made by your insurance company regardless of who is at fault. Collision does not, however, cover injuries to people or damage to the property of others.

Both comprehensive and collision are optional and are usually sold with a *deductible.* The deductible is the loss, or discount, you agree to pay whenever you file a claim. In other words, you pay the deductible before the insurance coverage kicks in. The deductible, in effect, protects the insurer against petty claims. The higher the deductible, the lower the premium. Increasing your deductible from $100 to $500 (absorbing or paying the first $500 of a claim) can lower your collision premium by as much as 35 percent. A $1000 deductible will save you 60 percent.

A similar deductible is available on collision insurance and is one of several key ways to limit the high cost of automobile insurance. What you must bear in mind here is that by carrying a high deductible, you are essentially "insuring yourself" by assuming some of the burden of the insurer. The greater the burden you assume, the lower the carrying costs on the policy will be. More on the pros and cons of self-insuring in a moment. Now let's go on to the three supplementary coverages listed, which provide important protections.

Three Supplementary Options

The three remaining automobile coverages available are *medical payments, uninsured motorists,* and *no-fault insurance.*

Medical payments is the medical insurance you carry (for yourself and your family or guests in your car) over and above any medical plan (or injury liability) you might already carry. Unlike injury liability coverage, medical payments insurance covers your medical expenses regardless who is at fault in any given accident.

Uninsured motorist coverage protects you and your car against hit-and-run drivers, drivers who carry no liability insurance, and (in almost all states) insured drivers whose insurance companies become insolvent. Some insurers offer this coverage in the form of both bodily injury and property damage. Others offer it for bodily injury alone. If you already carry adequate medical insurance, you may decide to pass on the bodily injury coverage component. But what about property damage to your vehicle? Suppose that the car's book value is $10,000 and that you've decided to keep it in mint condition. Because of its high book value, let's say you carry comprehensive and collision, but with a high deductible in order to keep your premium down. Is additional protection really necessary? Probably not, since all damage to your car is already covered under your existing insurance, regardless of circumstances. It depends on where you live—your state, your neighborhood, local law enforcement standards, and the other drivers you share the roads with.

For example, if your state's liability laws are still fairly new and just catching on, insuring against this kind of property damage by uninsured motorist coverage may be a good idea, especially if uninsured motorists are common in your area. In the event of an accident involving a hit-and-run or uninsured driver, your collision policy will already pay the damages to your car—*less the deductible* that you've selected. But its big advantage over collision only is that uninsured motorist insurance has *no deductible.* That is, it pays in full without any penalty. With high-deductible collision coverage, you might absorb the loss rather than file a claim, whereas with uninsured motorist coverage there's little reason not to go ahead and file. But here again, there a lot of ifs.

One of the ifs is that you will probably not be able to collect on your uninsured motorist coverage unless you can *prove* the at-fault (other) driver was uninsured. You have a good chance of collecting if you happen to witness the accident yourself and exchange all the necessary information with the other driver. Your best bet, however, is to call the police to the scene of the accident, no matter how minor the damage. Otherwise it's probably your word against the at-fault driver's when your insurer tries to collect damages.

An appropriate example was recently inscribed on the side of our car by an uninsured motorist. Although Texas has stiff car insurance laws, they're fairly recent, and some motorists are still lax in observing them. Accordingly, we decided early on that the minor expense of uninsured motorist coverage might be money well spent. Sure enough, only a few weeks into the policy, a vintage driver of a 1964 Chevy Impala wiped the side off of our parked car, creating a $600 repair bill in body parts, trim, and paintwork. Fortunately, one of us witnessed the accident and ran after the 15-mph hit-and-run motorist at the next stop sign. The driver was unable to produce proof of insurance,

134

so I took down what information there was, documented the accident from several angles with Polaroid photographs, and drove immediately to our neighborhood substation. After filing an accident report verifying the damages, I reported the police case number to our insurance agent—all this promptly within the hour. Even so, our insurer was unable in the long run to collect from the at-fault driver, who successfully contested the accident because the police had not been called to the scene.

We'll cover other ifs in the section "When and When Not to File a Claim."

No-fault insurance is a relative newcomer to the still evolving insurance industry. So far it exists, in one form or another, in only 22 states. No-fault covers medical and hospital expenses, regardless who was at fault. It can in some instances also cover the loss of income following an accident, but with few exceptions it does *not* cover damages to anyone else's property. No-fault, then, allows accident victims to recover hospitalization and medical costs (and perhaps even lost income) from *their own* insurer rather than waiting out the lengthy settlement period usually involved in trying to collect from another company. An advantage to no-fault is that it cuts through legal red tape following an accident and speeds up insurance settlements by deferring the testy and often disputed question, Who was at fault?"

Another feature of no-fault insurance is that it limits the conditions under which lawsuits are permitted. No-fault insurance evolved as a reaction to the difficult and time-consuming process of determining who was at fault, and thus legally liable, when an accident occurred. Too many people were suing and being sued on the basis of inconclusive evidence, jury awards were inconsistent (higher than actual losses in some instances, lower or nonexistent in others), and settlements were endlessly delayed by appeals or other time-consuming litigation. No-fault laws have dramatically reduced, if not eliminated, the number of frivolous court cases and have sped up the payment process for medical expenses, rehabilitation, and wage-loss compensation. Because no-fault insurance is regulated by the state, there are significant variations in the amount of coverage mandated from one state to another. Only New Jersey and Michigan have no "cap," or payment limit, on medical payments. In other states, medical payments and and wage-loss coverage is evaluated against existing health and disability coverages carried by the policyholder. The latter practice recognizes that additional no-fault insurance is less essential where adequate health and liability coverage already exist.

Among the important variations in no-fault found from state to state are these:

- A cap on medical and funeral expenses
- A cap on essential services payments (wages paid to anyone providing services that an unsalaried homemaker cannot provide)
- Limits on the right to sue (usually set at death, permanent injury, or disfigurement and a specific amount of medical cost—the so-called threshold for suit).

In some states that have no-fault laws, you may elect to pass on the *personal injury protection* (PIP) part of the package—the expanded medical payments coverage that compensates for lost wages as well as hospital bills. If you decide against PIP, you may be required to sign a waiver forfeiting that coverage. PIP protection reduces, but does not eliminate, the need for increased personal injury liability over and above the usual required limits. The basic requirements for bodily injury and property liability still apply under the laws governing no-fault insurance, and depending on what you personally stand to lose, you should still raise your liability protection in order to be adequately covered. Finally, if you do carry PIP and are involved in an accident in which you are not at fault, you may be able to claim both bodily injury liability from the other party and PIP from your own insurer and thus collect *double insurance* on the same accident.

Table 7.1 provides a summary of no-fault coverages published by the Insurance Information Institute, a highly regarded nonprofit information and action center that monitors the insurance industry. The information in the

Table 7.1 Summary of No-Fault Coverages

Bodily injury	Policyholder	Other Persons
Bodily injury liability	No	Yes
Medical payments	Yes	Yes
Uninsured motorists	Yes	Yes
Property damage		
Property damage liability	No	Yes
Comprehensive physical damage	Yes	No
Collision	Yes	No

table is generalized but will nevertheless improve your understanding of what no-fault does and doesn't cover. If you need additional general information on this subject, write to the Insurance Information Institute at 110 William Street, New York, NY 10038, or phone their hotline: 800/221-4954.

Getting the Best Coverage for the Money

Insurance companies arrive at their rating structure through what they term "loss experience" analyses. It's a complicated process, the net result of which is that the cost of insurance premiums can differ for exactly the same coverage from one company to another or from one part of a state to another. Likewise, no two people will be offered the exact same deal, even by the same insurance company. There are just too many variables that insurers have to take into account—your age, your sex, your driving record, your present insurer, and your physical condition, just to start. Other considerations that bear on the industry's definition of you as a "viable risk" include your marital status, the make and model car you drive, the area you live in, and where the car will be parked (in a garage or on the street). The list goes on and on, resulting eventually in a "driver profile" and a "risk classification." For instance, a male driver, 21 years old and unmarried, can pay up to three times more than the 35-year-old married neighbor who drives the same make and model car. That's because the 21-year-old male fits the profile of the insurance industry's highest "risk experience" group. (Some people question the constitutionality of the industry's bias against unmarried males under 25.) But regardless of the "risk experience" category you're in, if you're just beginning to shop around for an affordable insurance policy and a reliable insurer, the following pointers will start you off on the right foot:

- If insurance is mandatory, look beyond the minimum requirement, which is probably not enough. Instead, buy the amount of insurance *you need.*
- If it's optional, buy it *only if you need it* and buy only as much as you need.
- Shop around—compare insurers and the deals they offer you. Then decide which one is best.
- Go with one of the major insurers, a company with a known track record rather than the lowest bidder.

Use your Yellow Pages to identify the scores of companies offering car insurance, and contact a wide number of them for quotes. Here's where a lot of people come up short. After making a few phone calls, they tire of comparison shopping. According to the National Insurance Consumer Organization (NICO), fewer than one in four people even calls a second company or agent or compares quotes when shopping for car insurance. You can do better than that and save money in the process. Check the track record and the rating policies of the companies you're interested in. For example, all insurance companies divide states into "rating territories." A territory rated as high-risk by one company may be rated less so by another. In addition, some state insurance departments make customer complaint records available upon request. State regulatory agencies specify that insurance rates must be adequate, not unfairly discriminatory, and not excessive. If your quoted premium seems high, your insurer may be required to declare in writing that "the premium charged for this policy is greater than the premium rate promulgated by the state board of insurance"—and that's a tip-off that further comparison shopping is in order. A declaration such as this stamped on our car insurance renewal notice a few years ago prompted us to do some more comparison shopping. As a result we shaved $150 off our premium, even while adjusting some of our deductibles downward.

There is no question that some companies are a lot more expensive than others, often by as much as 50 percent. By shopping around you'll probably find that your driver classification (and your premium) will vary appreciably. Some of the larger companies often prove to be the least expensive. Nationwide, Allstate, and State Farm are what is known as "direct writers." They keep their costs down by operating their own sales forces. Aetna and Travelers may not be more expensive, although the independent agents who market their product do take home higher sales commissions.

Least expensive of all are probably the companies that sell insurance by mail and toll-free numbers rather than through agents. Among the better known of these are Amica Mutual, USAA, and GEICO. To be accepted by Amica Mutual you must be recommended in writing by a member policyholder and have a good driving record. USAA only insures retired officers of the armed services. GEICO (Government Employees Insurance Company) is accessible to the general public (you don't have to be a government employee to qualify). GEICO is the fifth largest of the nation's 1000 stockholder-owned auto insurance companies. Like Amica Mutual and USAA, GEICO's direct sales approach cuts out the middleman, benefiting the consumer in the form of lower premiums. As a group, they have an outspoken policy of insuring only "good drivers."

If for some reason you've been placed in your state's "assigned risk" pool, you needn't bother to apply to any of them. Moreover, if you drive an expensive "high-risk" car—a Jaguar or a BMW will do—you may be turned down flat by these cost-cutting companies, regardless of your spotless driving record. But if you do qualify and are accepted by one of them, you'll save substantially without sacrificing such vital requirements as fair evaluations and prompt claims settlements, both high priorities on any policyholder's list.

How Much Coverage Should You Buy?

The question "How much should I buy?" is stickier with comprehensive and collision coverage than with liability coverage. Remember, the first two are coverages you're not required to have, the ones that protect *your* car. Liability is simpler. Because it's usually mandatory, the question becomes "How much above the required minimum should I buy?" Liability, you will recall, is the insurance that protects you from legal action by (and potentially devastating court awards to) the other party. Put very simply, your liability coverage should match a worst-case situation, based on the vulnerability of your assets in the event of a high court award against you. Awards of $1 million are still uncommon but increasing: There were 30 million-dollar settlements in 1982, 49 in 1984.

Liability, then, is not something you'll want to skimp on. State minimum requirements are generally inadequate, and the cost of doubling or tripling this minimum requirement is relatively low. For a modest 8 to 11 percent increase in premium (say, $20 a year), you can probably increase your liability coverage from $100,000 to $300,000 per accident. Beyond that, if you happen to have substantial assets or earnings to protect, you might consider either a *single-limit policy*, which pays a flat amount, say, $300,000, per accident, including property damages, regardless of how many people are involved, or, for even higher coverage, an *umbrella policy*, which takes over where your home and car liability insurances end and provides $1 million of protection for as little as $100 a year.

The amount of comprehensive and collision coverage you should buy is an issue raised by an agent eager to make a sale. A more fundamental question should come first: "Do I need either?"

Depending on the car you drive, you may not. If you drive a three-year-old American car, the book value is probably only one-third the original price —and book value, or current market price, is what your insurance will pay if the car is stolen or "totaled" in an accident. Insure it? Maybe! But if your car is older than three years, it is probably not worth what it would cost you to carry comprehensive or collision at all. You must weigh the cost of protecting your vehicle against what it would cost *you* to replace it. Obviously, if your car is a limited-edition collector's item, comprehensive and collision insurance represents good value for money. Even so, you might want to lower your carrying costs by raising your deductible—the amount you are willing to "kick in" up front on any claim. Remember, increasing your deductible from $100 to $500 will save you about 35 percent with most companies. If you're willing to gamble that you won't be at fault and that the required minimum property damage liability carried by the other party will cover the value of your car, a $1000 deductible will bring your collision premium down as much as 60 percent.

The bottom line on comprehensive and collision is to insure your own car for its book value only, and put resulting savings back into insuring against the more important risks of a major personal injury or devastating property liability settlement. As the following illustration shows, if you drive an easily replaced old clunker, you're better off self-insuring—that is, not buying comprehensive and collision coverage.

An example of a borderline car from the standpoint of insurance is the one the kid next door is about to inherit on his nineteenth birthday. Andrew M.'s dad is ready to sign over the old 1981 Chevy Citation to his son and pick up the insurance premium as long as Andrew keeps up his grades at college and carries the car insurance in his own name. The offer is for liability coverage only, but Andrew wants to insure his first car to the hilt. "What happens if a parking lot attendant totals it?" he asks his dad. Mr. M. quotes book value to his son. With 83,000 miles on the clock, the car is worth, at best, $1800. The cost of insuring it would be disproportionate to its replacement value, even if Andrew, as a "youthful operator," were to be excluded from the policy:

Comprehensive with $100 deductible	$ 95
Collision with $200 deductible	193
Optional insurance total	$288

But with Andrew as the insured driver, the comprehensive remains the same, and collision jumps dramatically:

Comprehensive (same deductible)	$ 95
Collision (for youthful operator)	770
Defensive driving discount	− 77
Optional insurance total	$693

On learning that he will have to self-insure the old Citation, Andrew asks, "Self-insure? What's that?" "That's keeping both hands on the wheel when you're driving and the key in your pocket when you're not," his dad tells him.

Self-insuring may not be the gamble Andrew thinks. The statistics on road accidents are on his side. According to figures recently released by the Highway Loss Data Institute, only 10 percent of the cars on the road in any one year will be involved in accidents serious enough to file a collision claim. With a little extra care, Andrew's "old clunker" will easily last him through college.

When and When Not to File a Claim

Let's say you do carry collision and file an at-fault claim. You can basically add the cost of doing so to your next year's premium. Some insurance companies are more lenient than others, but all will levy an average surcharge of 20 percent if you file an at-fault claim of as little as $400. This surcharge on accidents *caused by the insured* is approved by your state insurance board and is something to bear in mind when deciding who pays for an accident, you or the insurer. Of course, if you were *not* at fault, the at-fault party pays. But if you crunched your car while running a stop sign and then claim for repairs, your insurer will up your premium the allowable 20 percent, an amount disproportionate, in many cases, to the cost of paying for the $400 repair yourself. To put it another way, by keeping your deductible high, you're much more apt to absorb such a small claim yourself and guard your low premium by doing so.

Comprehensive claims, by contrast, are not "surchargeable," and your premium will not be increased, regardless of how many claims you file. However, if you file an "unusual" number of claims in an allotted time period, your insurance company will instead simply fail to renew your policy when it reaches the expiration date. In other words, there is a unofficial limit on the number of times you can exercise your claim rights on comprehensive coverage. Again, it's not so much a dollar limit as it is a repeated-use limit. You should therefore avoid filing nuisance claims (as for stolen hubcaps) and save your comprehensive coverage for more substantial losses. Again, the way to

141

do this is to carry a higher deductible to start with. In any case, you can probably file at least three claims in an 18- to 20-month period without jeopardizing your insurance renewal rates.

Looking for the Discounts

There's another way to keep your car insurance costs down. Many insurance companies offer 5 to 30 percent discounts to customers who qualify on certain risk-reducing merits. Not all discounts are offered by every company or in every state, so you'll have to check with your agent as to which ones you qualify for.

- *Driver training and defensive driving courses*—these apply to high school–age drivers who have passed state-approved driver education programs and to drivers who have taken special defensive driving courses offered in certain localities under the supervision of qualified instructors.
- *Passive restraints*—such as self-activated seat belts or air bags that provide automatic protection.
- *No-claims bonuses for accident-free drivers*—usually available to drivers who have a clean record of at least three years.
- *Low-milage drivers and car-pool members*—available to those whose annual mileage is under average—typically 7500 miles or less (worth 10 percent in some states).
- *Antitheft devices*—burglar alarms or antitampering devices that immobilize the car unless the ignition key is used (described later in this chapter).
- *Other discounts are available for senior citizens* (over the age of 60 or 65), *women* between the ages of 30 and 65, *good students* (high school or college students with a B or better average), *farmers* (who drive in unpopulated areas), *nonsmokers, nondrinkers, and multi-car families* (each car costing less to include on the policy), and the *car you drive.* Your agent can give you the names of cars that most insurance companies prefer to (and not to) insure. Certain cars (imported, high-performance, sporty, especially if painted bright red) are considered poor insurance risks.

Discounts such as these can really save you a tidy sum, even if you have to take a defensive course or install passive restraints in your car to become

142

eligible. Driver education is an especially good choice for young people just beginning to drive. Not only will their insurance rates go down on completion of the course, but safety educators and insurance companies all agree that formally trained drivers are involved in fewer accidents than those who are taught by a friend or family member. You should note that by adding noncertified drivers to your policy, you can automatically forfeit your discount in many states. Insurance companies generally require that all parties listed on a discounted policy be certified as defensive drivers if the discount is to remain in force. Finally, some courts offer drivers the option of enrolling in a driver education program in lieu of paying a fine.

Specialty Insurance

This is another area that the modern consumer of car insurance can explore—towing, replacement car rental, stolen radios (if excluded from your comprehensive), accident coverage available through automobile club memberships, and so on. Although relatively inexpensive, these optional coverages are seldom called upon and, when they are, usually prove inadequate. A $20- or $25-a-year towing policy, for example, usually pays only a fixed amount over and above the labor charges at the scene of the breakdown, plus a flat $50 for towing your car away. The consensus on this kind of coverage is that it is insurance against inconvenience rather than against serious economic consequences. That's not to say you necessarily shouldn't carry it. If your work life, for example, is linked to your personal automobile, $15 or $20 a year or a replacement rental vehicle might pay for itself in the peace of mind that comes with guaranteed mobility. Finally, if you already carry car insurance, the optional coverage offered by car rental agencies is unnecessary. Rental car insurance is generally a poor buy and should be avoided unless you have reason not to involve your insurer (as when you've already reached your allotted limit on comprehensive claims) should an accident occur when you're driving a rental car.

Car Security Systems

Protecting your car with some kind of security device is closely related to your insurance protection. A security system on your car that qualifies for a discount can significantly cut the cost of your premium. Some insurance companies freely offer such discounts, while others are not permitted by state law to do so. Table 7.2 lists major companies and the discounts they offer

Table 7.2 Antitheft Device Discounts Offered by Seven Major Insurers

Company	Discount (%)
Liberty Mutual	10–15
Allstate	5–30
Travelers	5–20
State Farm	5–15
Farmers	5–15
USAA	5–15
GEICO	5–10

qualifying policyholders on the comprehensive portion of their premium.

Car security systems are ranked for insurance purposes according to how much protection they offer and the means by which they are activated, whether passively or by the operator of the vehicle. To qualify for a insurance discount, a security system on a car usually must be passive, which is to say, completely automatic. If the system is operator-activated, either with a key or a numerical code entered in a keypad, it will probably not qualify for a discount with most companies.

Moreover, the kind of car protection most insurance companies want to see will incorporate an antitheft device that, in addition to being passive, does something concrete to deter theft. A model security system for insurance discount purposes will generally include self-buckling seat belts or an air bag, an automatic hood lock, an electronic (rather than mechanical) alarm, and a disabling device that makes it difficult to move the car under its own power. These disabling devices usually deactivate either the ignition or the fuel supply and incapacitate the vehicle for anyone who tries to operate it without first disengaging the system.

If you're only interested in bare-bones security for your car and not in qualifying for an insurance discount, what you're talking about is an *alarm device* that broadcasts a distress signal, backed up by a *hood lock* (to prevent battery disconnection and "hot wiring" of the ignition), a sensor device such as a *motion detector* (to respond to jacking, bumping, or towing movements), or similar devices that pick up minute fluctuations in electrical current (as when an open door turns on the interior lights). Among the ever-growing number of options are *piezoelectric sensors* (to detect breaking glass), *pagers* (to activate a pocket beeper), and miniaturized *remote controls* (small enough to fit on a key chain). The remote controls include *disarming devices*

144

that enable you to reenter the car without triggering the alarm, complete with adjustable delays (on passive models only) that allow you to program the lag time between entering the car and punching in your access code.

What Does All This Cost—and Is It Really Worth It?

A *nonpassive alarm device* that offers minimum protection and includes an entry delay timer can be bought for $150 or less. Alternatively, you can get a combination *hood lock and starter ignition or fuel system disabling device* costing anywhere from $150 to $1000, depending on the options. It's not uncommon for luxury cars to carry special security systems that exceed the $1000 mark. Some American carmakers are now offering factory- or dealer-installed passive systems in their top-of-the-line models. On average, these optional features push up the sticker price by about $250. The key chain remote control transmitter, starting at around $500, is the most expensive single component on the market.

But before you go out and start spending money, there are many preventive measures you can take that protect your car and cost you nothing. You should already be practicing these before acquiring an array of high-tech gadgets to back you up.

- Close the windows and lock the car each time you leave it.
- Turn the wheels toward the curb and lock the steering.
- Leave the emergency brake on and the car in gear or in "park" (to make towing difficult).
- Lock important documents in the glove compartment or, better still, take them with you.
- Never leave anything behind in the car that will draw anyone's attention to it.
- Leave only your ignition key with parking lot attendants, not a key chain full of keys.
- Garage your car, if possible, or park it in well-lit places.

You can also etch the 17-character vehicle identification number (VIN) of your car on the corner of each window using a stenciling tool and acid etching solution. Thieves are cost-conscious. Although the numbers are inconspicuous, thieves would still have to replace all the glass before they could sell the car. The sight of the numbers etched on the windows might be enough to send them looking elsewhere. The same number etched on your hubcaps will serve the same purpose.

Next, take a careful look at your car's book value. If the car is high on the shopping list of car thieves, it's probably already well insured. So make sure it merits the extra expense on top of your comprehensive coverage, the insurance under which the security system qualifies for a discount. If it does, go ahead and make it as difficult to steal as possible. Car theft is at the top of the property crimes list in the United States today, and it's showing no signs of slowing down. Although it wasn't stolen, our car (not equipped with a security device) was broken into on a recent trip to a high car-crime area. We parked in a lot for *four minutes* at the Cloisters in New York City's Fort Tryon Park—just long enough to take a turn around the outside of the museum (we knew not to leave it there to go inside). In the course of our brief walk we lost a window, a Blaupunkt stereo and the section of the dashboard it fits into, and the contents of the glove compartment. The experience reminded us that some break-ins can be prevented, or at least stopped at the glass-breaking stage, by an audible alarm device. At no time were we out of earshot of the parking area. (It also reminded us that the trademark on our BMW stands for "break my window.")

If your car is really worth the cost of protecting it, remember that there's no guarantee that a professional thief who wants it badly enough won't get it anyway. Unless what you stand to gain (in either dollars saved or personal safety) is proportionate to your added protection costs, you might well forgo a car security system. Another important point is that there are a few security devices on the market that can do more harm than good if not used properly. For example, if an ignition disabling device is defective or is installed improperly, it can shut off the engine and the power steering. If you happen to be on a busy highway when this happens, your security device could cost you your life. By the same token, an improperly functioning fuel line cutoff device might allow the car to reach the open road before starving the fuel flow to the engine. If your car then stalls and causes an accident, even if you're not hurt, you're still legally liable for any injury or damage that might result. Finally, a silent paging device that broadcasts a break-in warning can be dangerous, or fatal, if the owner rather than the police responds to the call and takes an armed criminal by surprise.

Nevertheless, experts predict that by the 1990s most cars will come with factory-installed antitheft devices of one kind or another. Already, new mi-

146

croprocessor systems with more "discriminating" sensors are standard equipment in certain production makes and models. The next generation of onboard computers will disable ignition circuitry (for everyone except the car owner) by responding only to a factory-encoded "access number." Standard equipment in cars of the future will include tape cassette–sized "smart transceivers" that broadcast a signal and lead the police to the hiding place if and when the car is stolen.

If you've determined that your car warrants the extra protection of a security system, visit your local security or auto parts store, where you will find a wide variety of the easy-to-install products selling at prices well under those offered by car dealers. Also check the Yellow Pages under Burglar Alarm Systems or Locks and Locksmiths. Another good source of advice on installing electronic security devices is your stereo dealer, who understands the relationship between your car's electrical system and the components of a security system. And don't forget, if your insurance company offers one of the higher discounts for security system installation, say, 15 to 25 percent, your savings on the premium alone may pay for a *passive (keypad-operated) starter cutout,* which experts agree is the safest (because it won't leave you stranded while the car is in motion) and also the least costly of car disabling devices—between $120 and $180, including installation.

Summary

While it's true that the cost of car insurance, like everything else, is going up from one year to the next, the benefits and services being offered are also being refined and improved by state regulatory agencies and consumer organizations such as NICO and the Insurance Information Institute. Still, it is up to each of us to negotiate the best car insurance deal we can get. There's ample latitude for comparison shopping. So remember these points:

- Have a clear idea of what you're looking for when you start your comparison shopping for car insurance. That way you're less open to persuasion and more apt to buy only what you need.
- Bear in mind that the average policyholder is overinsured on collision (overprotecting the car owned) and underinsured on liability (underprotecting against catastrophic personal injury and property losses).

- Stick to the majors—Nationwide, Allstate, State Farm, Amica Mutual, GEICO, Travelers, Farmers, Aetna, Liberty Mutual, and several others. Bargain insurance is no bargain if the company goes out of business, consistently contests claims, or handles them slowly.
- Don't switch around if you find a company you're happy with. A company that you have an accident-free five-year record with is less apt to increase your premium after your first at-fault claim.
- Comparison shopping, including shopping for discounts, can save as much as 50 percent on your premium.

Finally, remember that the primary purpose of insurance of any kind is to protect you and your family from catastrophic financial loss—from a debilitating injury or legal judgment that could literally cost you the roof over your head, your savings, your future income, or a combination of them all. Seen on this scale, the loss of a car (even a Rolls-Royce Silver Cloud with platinum door handles) is never truly catastrophic. Your annual outlay on insurance premiums should always be weighed against the relative worth of what you stand to lose. If the balance between the two is right, you're well within the parameters of total coverage.

Car Security Systems

The principal facts to keep in mind if you're considering a security system for your car are these:

- A car is stolen somewhere in the United States every 30 seconds. Chances are one in 44 that your car will be broken into *this year*.
- Only about half of the cars currently stolen are ever recovered (usually ones that have been abandoned by thieves and joyriders).
- Depending on the car you drive, a security system may or may not be a good consumer buy. When its relatively high cost is added to the insurance premiums you're already paying, a car security device ranks as a luxury rather than a necessity.
- Remember that a security system may deter a thief but will probably not absolutely prevent your car from being stolen. So before buying a high-tech system, be sure to tighten up your basic security: Keep the car locked and, if possible, garaged. When parking on the street, turn the wheels to the curb, lock the steering, and engage

the emergency brake. Leave nothing behind in the car that could invite a break-in.

- A car security system can, however, qualify you for a 5 to 30 percent insurance discount, depending on the insurer and the device installed. A discount of, say, 20 percent becomes a serious incentive to install a security device, especially if your insurance premiums are above average.

8

Basic Home Security

THERE IS A BURGLARY IN THE UNITED STATES EVERY TEN SECONDS. ONE HOME IN 12 WILL BE BURGLARIZED THIS YEAR.

POLICE REPORTS INDICATE THAT MORE THAN 60 PERCENT OF HOME BURGLARS ENTER THROUGH *UNLOCKED* DOORS OR WINDOWS.

STUDIES SHOW THAT DELAYING A BURGLAR *FOUR MINUTES* MAY BE ENOUGH TO MAKE HIM CALL OFF THE ATTEMPT.

These figures are convincing evidence that our homes, families, and possessions are underprotected from crime. In this chapter we will examine why this is so and spell out some of the basic precautions you can take to keep from becoming one of the more than 8 percent of Americans whose homes will be broken into this year. Even although the problem has reached epidemic proportions, there is a lot you can do to take your home off the list of likely targets in your neighborhood.

According to the National Crime Prevention Institute at the University of Louisville, homeowners across the country are making it too easy on burglars. Not only do 60 percent of our burglars walk in unopposed, another estimated 25 percent use little or no force—a swift kick on a nonreinforced door jamb, the twist of a $3 screwdriver inserted in a low-security lock. Figure it out for yourself. That leaves only 15 percent of our candidate burglars having to work at all to gain entry to our homes. Little wonder that the odds favor the burglar.

Developing a Security Action Plan

So what can you do to even up the odds a little? To start off, it helps to know whom you're dealing with. Don't kid yourself. The burglar knows who you are—when you come and go, what, if any, precautions you've taken to "harden the target," and how much trouble he'll have to go to to locate its weaknesses. Your typical burglar is probably male, in his mid to late teens, from your general neighborhood, and unskilled at breaking and entering. As an amateur, the only thing he has in common with his professional counterpart is a preference for disposable goods that are readily exchanged for hard cash—stereo components, TV and VCR equipment, personal computers, jewelry, furs, silver, expensive sports equipment, and the like.

The next step is to think the way the burglar does, to match his strategy with one of your own. This means coming up with a plan of action in which *you* are the first line of defense in protecting your home and the valuables you keep in it.

The first thing to realize is that, from the burglar's point of view, *time* is the worst enemy. Any obstacles you put in a burglar's path to slow him down will hinder his efficiency and probably make him think twice before choosing your home as a target. Your plan, then, must be to slow a burglar down by creating a simple but practical network of time-consuming deterrents, an "obstacle course" through which he must pass before breaching your fortifications. Four minutes is about all you need to make a burglar stop and reconsider his plan. After that he'll probably go find an easier job somewhere else.

Start by "casing" your property just like your burglar would. Study the operation as if your goals and his were the same. Assess the risk involved in gaining access to the property:

152

- Is the house or apartment self-contained?
- How many ground-level doors and windows are there?
- Is the property isolated, or is it in easy view of neighbors or passing traffic?
- Is the property fenced? Does it have a gate that locks?
- Are there signs of a security system (not just window stickers)?
- Are there other visible precautions—well-lit exterior, a guard dog?
- Is the area patrolled? How far is it to the nearest police station?
- Is there a quick escape route leading from the property?

Look for the obvious weak spots, through the burglar's eyes. Once you can pick them out—untrimmed shrubbery (to hide behind), unlocked garage or shed (handy supply of tools to use)—you can get on with setting up the necessary deterrents. The important thing at this stage is to match the deterrent to the risk, to the potential crime you wish to avoid. In other words, "hot properties" that burglars specialize in call for equally "hot" precautions in the way of tight security.

Putting Your Plan into Action

Securing a house or an apartment calls for equal parts common sense and practical knowledge of home security basics, starting with keys, doors, locks, windows, and lighting, moving on to general security improvements, inventory and property identification procedures, and insurance discounts, and finishing up with all-round neighborhood security. Given that an estimated 60 percent of all intruders enter through unlocked doors and windows, you need to start right there, tightening up obvious security soft spots first. The following survey of "hot" precautions is presented in the order in which home protection efforts usually go *wrong*.

House keys. It's with good reason then that house keys top the list of hot security precautions—not least because people forget to use them, leave them in the door lock after using them, misplace them, or simply lose them. Since keys enable the holder to enter the secured area, no questions asked, it's paramount that you do nothing to place your key in the hands of the wrong person. There are a number of ways burglars gain access to your house using keys—your keys, a pass key, or a key substitute. Maybe you lost your key chain with your identification on it. Did you turn your keys over to a commercial parking lot attendant? Did a repairman make himself a copy when you left him the keys to the house? Or maybe your lock accepts a master key—standard equipment for a lot of burglars. Or worse, could your old lock be so worn that any key, or even a sharp instrument, will turn the cylinder? If someone walks into your home that easily, you'll probably never know how it happened. The police may not even file a breaking-and-entering report because there is no sign of forced entry to the premises. So follow these commonsense guidelines:

- Don't keep more keys on hand than you actually need. Make up extra keys only as you need them.
- Never hand your keys over to anyone you don't know personally and trust completely.
- Never carry identification on your key ring.

As to the quality of lock-and-key system you use, we'll come to that in a moment.

Doors. Doors are the most obvious and direct point of access to your property. Because they open and close on hinges and depend on latches, bolts, and locks to fasten them, even heavy-duty doors are only as secure as *you* make them. All exterior entrances to your home should be equipped with 1¾-inch-thick fire-resistant solid-core wooden or, even better, metal doors. If you live in a high-risk area, consider replacing glazed or paneled doors or covering them with metal grillwork on the *inside.* Wooden doors in isolated apartment building hallways or those not easily visible from the street should be drilled and metal rods inserted around the locking mechanism to prevent anyone from sawing the lock out with power tools. The door itself should fit snugly in place and not have gaps around the edges where wrecking bars or other tools can be inserted.

The framework around the door is as important to security as the door itself. Metal door frames, like metal doors, are more resistant to physical force than wooden ones. Wooden door frames and the studs inside the walls behind them should be solidly reinforced with *hardwood* building materials. Ready-made wood frames available from suppliers and builders usually come in easier-to-work-with (and therefore easier to wreck) softwoods. (Contractors are not in the security business, and they look upon reinforced hardwood door frames and pry-resistant door jambs as "custom" work.) Before mounting a door in the frame, test the jamb area by applying force around the strike plate where the bolt on the lock seats into the door frame. If there is any movement at all, your door could be easily "sprung," rendering your expensive hardware devices useless.

Any movement around the jamb area must be eliminated. To do this, remove the fascia (outer covering) on both sides of the jamb and anchor the door frame to the house studs inside the wall, using long screws or carriage bolts. If there's a gap between the door frame and the studs behind the wall (there usually is), fill it with hardwood or metal shims. By making the surrounding structure solid, the door frame, which holds the strike plate, cannot be sprung away from the lock bolt when the door is locked.

Doors are mounted opening inward so that the hinge pins are inaccessible from the outside. All fastening hardware, including hinges, should be matched to the size and weight of the door—the heavier the better—and be of the highest standard. In addition to mounting the hinges properly, you might also choose hinges with "security studs," a feature that prevents the door from being lifted, even when the hinge pins are removed. You can accomplish the same thing with your existing hinges by removing the center screws from both sides of each hinge plate and replacing one of these with a steel pin inserted in the door frame. Leave ½ inch protruding from the wall hinge plate that mounts to the inside of the door frame. When the door closes, the pin will fit into the opposite hinge plate mounted on the door, making the door difficult to pry or lift out of the frame.

Finally, if you live in a rented apartment where modification of the internal wall structure isn't permitted, door reinforcement is still possible by mounting *butt hinges* on the inside of the door and door facing. Make sure to fasten such exposed hinges with beveled-headed carriage bolts installed by drilling and inserting the bolts from the outside—through the wall—to the inside of the door and door facing. This makes the hinge effectively a part of the wall itself, enabling it to withstand all but the strongest of forces. Because the bolt heads are exposed on the outside wall, it's essential that they be beveled to prevent anyone gripping, turning, or otherwise prying them off.

Locks. Because locks are the counterparts of keys, make sure you are the original keyholder to any locks you depend on for your security. In other words, if you move to an already locked premises, don't take any chances— *change the locks.* You never know how careful the previous keyholders were or how many extra keys there may be floating around.

Now comes the big question: which kind of lock to install. There are a number of kinds to choose from, the choice being a direct function of the degree of security they offer.

First, let's eliminate the kind of locks you don't want—including the kind frequently provided by developers in housing projects and apartment blocks. The most popular of these is the key-in-the-knob type. These are easily defeated by breaking off the entire knob, exposing the tumbler mechanism inside. Other locks to avoid are old-fashioned mortise locks, locks that use master keys, or locks with keys than can be duplicated easily. These can be opened by anyone who either buys a mass-produced master key or has a key cut to order at the corner hardware store.

Locksmiths and security experts alike recommend the *interconnected lockset,* a latch bolt (spring-loaded door catch) with a deadbolt just above it. The lockset, being interconnected, is "panicproof," meaning that you can open both locks from the inside by turning *one* knob. Like any lock with a removable cylinder, the lockset should be equipped with a flush-mounted *high-security cylinder* designed to resist prying, picking, and drilling. (More on cylinders in a moment.)

For additional security, a *second deadbolt* makes an excellent auxiliary lock when placed a foot or so away from your lockset. A good backup lock delays a burglar even more, leaving him no choice but to use brute force (and make a lot of noise) if he is to enter by the door. Again, these locks come with removable or built-in cylinders and are either flush-mounted with a vertical bolt and face-mounted strike or are installed in the usual way with a standard horizontal bolt and strike recessed in the door jamb.

Next, if you have glazed or paneled doors and are unable or unwilling to replace them, you'll want to consider installing a *double-cylinder* lock. This type lock can only be operated with a key. It is designed to keep anyone from reaching inside and turning the bolt by hand. Thus it is not "panicproof" —the locking mechanism locks you *in* as well as out. The gain in security must therefore be weighed against the potential hazard when needing a key to get out quickly in an emergency.

In high-risk urban areas where maximum protection is essential, a "police lock" (manufactured by Fox) or a center-locking double sliding bar (by Multi-Lock) is recommended. The so-called police lock braces the door with a removable steel rod that slots into the lock housing on one end and anchors against the floor on the other. The "double slider" consists of opposable steel bars that shunt horizontally into heavy-duty fittings on either side of the door frame. This high-security lock is easily recognized from outside the locked

156

area by the unusual position of the cylinder in the center of the door. Since it, too, works on the double-cylinder principle, this lock is likewise not panic-proof and must be used with caution. These locks are rarely stocked by locksmiths and may have to be ordered (by a *dealer only*) from a wholesale distributor.

Glass sliding patio doors and the locks that come with them were not designed with security in mind and are easily broken into. The best, although far from adequate, protection is provided by metal accordion grills that slide across the opening in guide tracks like the one the doors fit in. To prevent sliding doors from being lifted out of their tracks, insert sheet metal screws into the top track above the door. Run the screws in until they barely clear the door top. To make the door stationary in its track, you can drill a hole through both the door and track frame and insert a metal pin (a nail will do) through both the door and the track, anchoring them together. You can also drop a length of rod or a broom handle into the floor of the track, obstructing the slot the door slides into.

If your garage connects with your living area, install the same kind of deadbolt lock on the door entering the house from the garage as you would on any other exterior door. Once inside the garage, a burglar can usually gain access to your dwelling without concerning himself about being seen by anyone.

Replacing doors, reinforcing door frames, and changing locks can be an expensive proposition. An unornamental high-security mahogany door costs between $65 and $95. The cost of reinforcing a door frame is not determined by materials so much as by the time it takes to do the work. The only expensive hardware will be the hinges themselves, the best grade costing $25 to $35 a set. No great skill is required, so if you prefer, you can do the work yourself and save the labor charges (two or three hours) a carpenter would invoice you for.

Good *two-lock sets* cost between $70 and $110, a single *auxiliary dead-bolt* about the same. Add a *high-security strike plate* ($15 to $20), a *lock cylinder guard plate* ($11 to $18), and a built-in through-the-door *peep-hole* for checking outside before opening the door ($15 to $25), and you've laid out the better part of $500 for starters. As for patio doors, *sliding-door locks* ($5 to $15) are designed especially for that purpose, but you should consider using one of these only in conjunction with a vertical-bolt auxil-iary lock for extra protection. For even further protection, the Fox and Multi-Lock double-bar-type locks retail for somewhat in excess of $100 each but are hard to beat if you don't mind living with all that hardware.

Here's a final checklist on locks:

- Make sure cylinder heads are shielded or equipped with tapered collars (to keep them from being vise-gripped and twisted off).
- Strike plates must accept a deep bolt—preferably 1 inch long (½-inch bolts can be too easily sprung).
- Bolts should have a hardened metal pin inside or, better, a rolling center that spins on contact with a hacksaw blade.
- Heavy-duty plates ("bodyguards") around cylinders give added protection, as do L-shaped shields ("jimmy guards") over strike plates, preventing pointed tools from being inserted between the door and the frame.

Of course, a fancy pick-resistant locking system does little good if you fail to use it. People we know went away for the weekend, forgetting to lock the otherwise high-security rear door to their home. Early Saturday evening their neighbors were puzzled to see a pizza delivery van come and go. Surmising that the occupants had returned early, they gave it no more thought. Later they learned that burglars had essentially moved in for the weekend and made the most of the accommodations before cleaning the house out completely.

Windows. Although sometimes used, windows are not the burglar's first choice for entering your home. Breaking glass is risky and noisy, and burglars like to avoid that whenever possible. Windows take more time to enter and leave by, and anyone doing so is conspicuous. To take advantage of these drawbacks, you should make sure your windows are as inaccessible and as exposed to view as possible. Offer the burglar no easy concealment or added protection such as high walls, fences, or shrubs to work behind. Force him to work out in the open where he can be seen by anyone passing by.

In tightening up your window security, concentrate on the more accessible windows first. Consider covering ground-level windows and windows on upper floors that can be reached from a roof or short ladder with sturdy iron grills. Metal accordion gates or hinged folding grills are the choice for windows you use as fire escapes. As a last resort, easily accessible windows located in out-of-the-way areas should be covered *permanently*—especially if you live in a high-crime area.

Both sash (sliding) and casement (hinged) windows can be temporarily fastened with a number of inexpensive devices—friction screws, wedges, and ventilating stops. An effective homemade way to secure sash windows is to drill and pin the window frames together with a nail that can be removed from the inside or with special screws commercially available for that purpose. Windows can be more permanently secured if equipped with locking devices—key-operated cams, key-operated pins, and specially designed window locks. A more expensive but highly effective procedure is to install high-security glazing—laminated plate glass or, less costly, glass with wire mesh in it to prevent it from being shattered.

Commercial sash screw kits with thumbscrews cost $5 to $6 a set. Casement window locks, such as those made by Ideal Security, retail for around $3. Laminated plate glass costs between $6 and $7 a square foot but may quickly pay for itself if installed a high-crime-area home.

Here are some other ways to tightening up window security:

- Replace windows glazed on the outside with interior-glazed windows.
- Cover all basement and garage windows with bars on the inside (especially if your garage is attached to your home).
- Place tables or other obstacles inside windows (passive "booby traps") to hinder the would-be intruder's mobility.
- Avoid turning your windows into a showcase of the household's contents.
- Do not regard storm windows and screens as part of your security system (with the exception of wired screens, one of the home security system components discussed in Chapter 9).

Lighting. Light is also high on the list of the burglar's enemies, following closely behind time and noise. That makes electrical lighting one of the most effective safety devices you can install in your home.

Let's start with outdoor lighting. The secret to good lighting is that it must be both bright and aimed directly at what *you* need to see. Used incorrectly, light can provide additional cover for intruders. Don't blind yourself, or helpful neighbors, by shining bright lights directly in their eyes. "Task lighting" (lighting with a specific purpose) should be directed at areas where an intruder will have to position himself in order to enter your home. So when hanging light fixtures, locate them well out of reach—high on a wall where no one can put them out of operation. And while you're at it, lock up your exterior breaker box and keep the area around it brightly lit.

Outdoor lighting fixtures can be controlled by automatic timers or photo-electric cells. The latter are self-regulating, but if you use automatic timers, make sure you adjust them to come on as soon as, but not before, darkness falls. That means changing the clock with the seasons. Nothing gives away an unoccupied house quicker than lights on during daylight hours when they're not needed. Automatic timers are an inexpensive solution to the problem. The kind you find in any hardware electrical department cost between $3 and $6. If your lights are not switched automatically, make sure you switch them on (and off) at appropriate intervals.

Concentrate on lighting these exterior areas:

- Each entrance to the house
- Ground-floor windows
- Porches, patios, and decks
- Incoming power terminal, meter boxes
- Front, back, and side yards
- Garage doors

Inside the home, the timing of lights going on and off at odd intervals is more important than what the lights themselves illuminate. In other words, indoor lighting should suggest activity, telling anyone who sees the house that it's probably occupied. If no one is home, timer-operated, photosensitive, or sound-activated lighting can still create the impression that someone is and that they're moving around inside. Rotating lights on timers is the key to keeping up your protection, especially when you're away. If you plan to be out late or away for a weekend, it's also a good idea to rig timers on other appliances, such as radios and electric fans.

Home lighting as a form of added security is more economical today than ever before. Old-fashioned incandescent lamps, which last 2000 hours and cost about 8 cents per kilowatt-hour to operate, can today be replaced by *high-pressure sodium* fixtures that last 24,000 hours and illuminate an area three times as large. Moreover, it's estimated by the manufacturers that sodium fixtures cost little more than $30 a year to operate. One example, the Guardsman (from Decra Home Products), lights a 7500-foot area with a single 70-watt bulb. It costs $125, a price the owner is said to recover in the first year of operation. There is, however, an aesthetic point to be made here. These primarily functional lights are often harsh and unflattering to the

160

appearance of your property. You may prefer to disregard the cost factor and use softer incandescents instead.

Another security-oriented lighting product that may prove useful, if your neighborhood or home is relatively quiet to start with, is a sound-activated fixture. Adjustable sensors inside the switch (wall outlet, wall switch, or screw-in bulb holder) pick up sound—footsteps, approaching automobiles, breaking glass—and turn on individual lights for short periods of time. One such product is the AudioLite (from Progressive Energy Corporation of Englewood, Colorado), which costs about $25. Other interior lights can be switched by standard automatic timers.

So much for projects that call for some knowledge of home security basics. With these so-called hot precautions taken care of, you're no longer a primary target for burglary. A few remaining details will tighten your defenses even more.

General Home Security Precautions

The following routine security measures, added to those you've already taken, will further reinforce your security base. These come under the heading of common sense and may therefore seem a little obvious. Perhaps they are—but not so obvious that everybody remembers to include them in their security action plans.

- Lock up your tools. Burglars who use *your* tools to break in are more difficult to prosecute.
- Trim tree branches that overhang roofs or reach near upper windows.
- Keep fences below eye level and hedges trimmed low. Obstruct the burglar on foot *but not your neighbor's view of him.*
- Keep the lawn mowed and garbage cans covered. (Lids off signal that you haven't been home since the last pickup.)
- Going away? Leave a car parked in the driveway. (Ask a neighbor to move garbage cans around and turn on a lawn sprinkler occasionally.)
- Stop mail and newspaper delivery or have someone remove these items regularly.
- Muffle ringing telephones or turn the volume down when you're away.

- Inform a ranking supervisor at the police precinct in your neighborhood when you're going and when you'll be back. (If you don't know him personally, get his name ahead of time. Although you occasionally hear of police burglars, the vast majority of the time the police are on your side.)

A special point or two about *telephone answering machines.* These handy devices are safer than a phone that goes on ringing forever, which can indicate that you're not home. Answering machines instead raise two questions: Are you not *home at the moment,* or are you unable to take the call? Your taped greeting should always suggest the latter but never explain that you can't take the call because you're not at home. Never confide, for example, "I'm out at the moment but will return your call as soon as I get back." Instead, simply say, "We're (implying that there are more than one of you) unable to take your call at the moment, so please leave your name and number and we'll get back to you shortly."

Also, there are some people around who use their telephone answering devices as a forum for making witty and ingenious statements about life. "Hello, this is Suzanne. So what's going on in your sweet head?" From the security standpoint, this seemingly innocent greeting sends the wrong message, attracting rather than warding off weirdos or people with criminally focused intentions. The burglar sees the telephone not as a private toy but as a public listening device, and there's nothing he'd rather hear than someone announcing to the world that she's "on another planet" but will return the call as soon as she gets back. Our advice, then, is that telephone answering devices be used to distance the user from potential threats and to keep that distance to a maximum. Preferably, this includes *not* offering the caller an explanation as to why your response is a recorded one. If you do leave a message explaining why you're unable to take the call, make sure you update it frequently, thereby communicating "activity on the premises" to the caller.

Making an Inventory of Your Home's Contents

The following material picks up where we left off earlier in the "contents endorsement" section of Chapter 6 where we discussed a household inventory with regard to replacement costs under homeowner's insurance coverage. From the home security standpoint, an inventory of your possessions

162

may not prevent you from losing them in a burglary, but it may help you recover them if they are stolen. In any case, in the course of itemizing your possessions one by one, you gain an awareness of what you stand to lose if you are the victim of a burglary, as well as what you might do to safeguard all these items from potential catastrophes of any kind.

As pointed out earlier, the documentation process consists of making a written record of each and every item of value, noting any identifying features (serial numbers, maker's marks, telltale flaws, etc.) that could help trace it if it were stolen or otherwise lost. The next step is to photograph the interior of your home room by room, showing all the major items listed. Items of special value should be photographed individually. Wherever possible, the photographs should provide visual evidence of special identifying features like wear and tear, trademarks, signatures, and the like. Another popular technique is to videotape the contents of your home, room by room, item by item, narrating with details as you do. Finally, in the unlikely event that your possessions are of exceptional value, your inventory could also be done by a licensed appraiser who will certify their worth for insurance purposes.

Speaking of insurance, you might note that some insurance companies offer a reduction in premiums for households that include the basic precautions enumerated at the beginning of this chapter. Under a typical state insurance code, State Farm, for example, offers a 5 percent discount to policyholders whose homes meet the following specifications:

- Exterior doors are 1⅜ inches thick, solid-core, and secured with deadbolt locks.
- Metal doors are secured with deadbolt locks.
- Double doors have the *inactive* door secured by header and threshold bolts that penetrate metal strike plates. If glass is located within 40 inches of the header and threshold bolts, these bolts are flush-mounted in the edge of the door.
- Sliding doors are secured by secondary locking devices to prevent lifting and prying.
- Garage doors are equipped with key-operated locking devices.
- Windows are secured by auxiliary locking devices.

To be eligible for this reduction in premiums, your home must first be inspected and then certified by a qualified public official. The crime prevention officer from your local police precinct is both a qualified inspector as well as a good source of advice if you wish to bring your home up to code.

Neighborhood Security

Working with your community and with your local police is an important part of your home security program. There are two basic things you can do to tighten up your own security in concert with your neighbors and local law enforcement officials:

- Participate in an Operation Identification program.
- Join a Neighborhood Crime Watch group.

Burglars count on you to be lax in your security measures, to make it easy on them to steal valuables that are easily converted to cash. The best way to hamper the burglar's "fencing" operation is to mark your valuables with an identification number. Your Social Security or driver's license number will do. Burglars caught with unmarked property are frequently released for lack of evidence. Marked property in the hands of a burglar will help the police make the charges stick and will help you get your stolen property back. That's why statistics show that homes that display the "Warning: Operation ID" sticker are at much less risk of burglary than those that don't.

Your local police, sheriff's office, or other law enforcement agencies usually have a simple *engraving tool* that they will lend you free of charge. In some areas, your local public library or other community groups and organizations offer the same service. The engraver is quick and easy to use. Make sure you place your ID number on part of the object not easily removed but preferably out of sight. Then make a list of objects bearing this number (or note this on your household inventory) and keep a copy in a safe place. You will then be given a window sticker that advertises your participation in this widely publicized program.

Another warning sign for the burglar scouting your neighborhood is a public notice that informs would-be offenders of the community's Crime Watch program. Police crime prevention units work with communities to organize watch groups on a street-by-street basis. Officers will gladly visit your home and evaluate your individual security needs. They will also attend meetings and offer advice on what to look for when keeping a watchful eye on one another's property, what constitutes unusual or suspicious behavior,

164

and what to do in case of a break-in. Studies show that burglary rates fall by as much as 60 percent in neighborhoods with well-organized Crime Watch programs.

Another advantage of a community Crime Watch program is that it brings you into closer contact with your local law enforcement agencies and lets them know that you appreciate the risks they routinely take on your behalf. This one-on-one with your local police might also speed up their response time if and when you phone in an emergency.

Summary

You may find that these practical and relatively inexpensive precautions are all you need in order to establish a perimeter of security around your home and your family. Let's hope so. This kind of security plan is one you can carry out in your spare time, and doing so needn't be a hassle. However, if you live in a high-risk area, you may need to look to more sophisticated and costly devices to safeguard your property and possessions. Without creating a home environment that rivals Fort Knox, there are devices and systems on the market that can be tailored to your individual needs; we'll come to those next. In the meantime, remember these key points about basic home security:

- Time, light, and noise are the principal deterrents to burglars. If you can slow them down, force them to work in bright light, and cause noise, they will probably move on to a less risky target.
- Other effective obstacles to put in the path of a burglar are solid-core doors, barred ground-level windows, and pry-, pick-, and drill-resistant deadbolt locks with vertical-bolt auxiliary locks as backups.
- Consider etching ID numbers on valuable personal property. Burglars will often pass over such highly traceable, difficult-to-dispose-of objects.
- These basic security steps may qualify you for a homeowner's insurance discount of 5 to 10 percent.
- Your security and protection largely depends on your personal efforts, but Neighborhood Crime Watch groups are also proven deterrents to neighborhood crime.

9

Home Security Systems

IN THE COMING YEAR, NEARLY 6 MILLION AMERICAN HOMES WILL BE BURGLARIZED.

NINETY PERCENT OF ALL BURGLARIES TAKE PLACE IN HOMES WITH EITHER NO SECURITY SYSTEM OR WITH ONE THAT'S NOT IN SERVICE AT THE TIME OF THE BREAK-IN.

All across America there is a need to combat the widespread wave of burglary, theft, and related violence sweeping the nation. According to figures released by a National Police Chiefs Conference, a burglary occurs somewhere in the United States every 10 to 15 seconds. Fortunately, public resistance is also growing in the form of increased vigilance and renewed determination to secure the home and "harden the target" for would-be burglars. So far about one in three homes in the nation has security devices of some kind in operation.

The security devices currently in use range from the basic implements and techniques described in Chapter 8—deadbolts with pick-resistant cylinders, sash window screws, and automatic lighting timers—to state-of-the-art electronic security systems, which are the subject of this chapter. What follows is a basic introduction to home security systems to help you narrow the field of choices and identify the kind of system that will best suit your security needs as well as your pocketbook.

Do You Need a Home Security System?

Home security is one of the hottest industries in America today. There are more than 12,000 independent alarm companies in the United States, including many well-known firms like Honeywell, Rollins, Brinks, ADT, Schlage, and Wells Fargo. Between them they offer everything from over-the-counter security products that anyone can install to technically complex systems complete with professional installation and 24-hour monitoring by the security company and even to a new and much simplified combination of the two, the owner-installed fully monitored system. With an ever-mutating inventory of security paraphernalia comes a bewildering glossary of microwave sensors, ultrasonic and passive infrared sensors, pressure mats, trip wires, remote-entry keypads, backup batteries, zone modules, and automatic telephone dialers, to mention just a few. But this array of hardware notwithstanding, the more basic question is, do you need a home security system at all? You probably would benefit from such a system if you meet any of the following conditions:

- You live in a high-crime area. For instance, rapidly changing urban neighborhoods undergoing "improvement" and affluent areas located in or close to major cities are among those frequently staked out by burglars. (In so-called bad neighborhoods, security systems are often ineffective because police response to them is less predictable. More on that shortly.)
- Your home has already been broken into. This unfortunately establishes you as an "easy mark," a "soft target" for area burglars.
- Your home is unoccupied during the day because both spouses have jobs or other activities outside the home or you travel a lot and are away nights as well.
- You are a woman or an older person living alone.
- Your home is isolated or otherwise not easily watched by neighbors or by passing vehicles.
- You have the kind of possessions burglars go for, items that are easily grabbed up and can be quickly converted to cash: electronic

168

equipment, silver, jewelry, furs, firearms, coin and stamp collections.

- You've taken all the routine security precautions discussed in Chapter 8 and still feel the need for more sophisticated protection.

If you still feel the need to add to your routine precautions, the first equipment you should install is a warning device that is closely related to home security systems.

Smoke Detectors

According to insurance experts, one fire is equal to a hundred burglaries in terms of losses suffered in a burned-out home. That's why a smoke detector is an essential part of any home protection system. Nowadays you have a choice of smoke-sensing equipment that works either independent of or integrated with a home security system.

Statistics compiled by the National Fire Protection Association reveal that the vast majority of fire fatalities and injuries in the United States occur in homes not equipped with *working* smoke detection devices. Since early warning is what smoke detectors are meant to provide, a slow-responding or dirt-clogged detector or a detector with a weak or dead battery is no detector at all.

There are two kinds of smoke detectors, and a well-protected house will have either one of each or a double-system unit that combines the two types in one.

- *Photoelectric smoke detectors* have a light source and a photoelectric cell, or "eye," housed in a dual chamber. The light-sensitive eye triggers the alarm only when smoke enters the open chamber and deflects light toward the photo cell.
- *Ion smoke detectors* have a clear air chamber in which slightly radioactive materials conduct a constant electrical current to a pair of electrodes. An alarm is triggered when smoke particles enter the chamber and interrupt the current flowing between the electrodes.

The need for the double system arises because different kinds of fires cause ion and photoelectric detectors to respond at different speeds. To register smoke and sound an early warning from both smouldering and

169

flaming fires, it's advisable to use both systems or a combination unit. There are fewer photoelectric detectors on the market to choose from, and even fewer combination units. You may have to shop around to find them, but at least two companies, First Alert and Sears, offer combination units nationally.

Features to look for in smoke detectors include a *low-battery indicator,* a *test button,* and an alarm *volume button* to hush the alarm temporarily if it goes off accidentally. Smoke alarms aren't expensive. A good one will cost between $25 and $40—although some security companies offer ion units that cost nearly double that amount when included in their burglar alarm package. Another noteworthy difference between makes and models of smoke detectors is the manufacturer's *warranty,* which can range from three months to five years.

If you install your smoke detector yourself, make sure you locate it away from fireplaces, kitchens, carports and garages, oil lamps, furnace exhausts, even laundries and bathrooms where moisture particles can set off false alarms. Moreover, you may have to screen the sensor chamber from insects that can get inside and set it off. You should have at least one smoke detector for each floor level of your home, located within easy earshot of the bedrooms.

Living with a smoke detector is good training for living with a security system. "Nuisance" alarms occur occasionally with both, but both can save you serious loss of property and, more important, life itself. These devices operate either independently or in liaison with one another via a 24-hour monitoring service. Exactly how central monitoring works will be seen in a moment. For now let's just say that fire and/or burglar alarm systems are seldom ever connected directly to local emergency services (except in some rural areas) but are instead monitored by either homeowners or professional security services.

A "No-Glitch" Security System

Let's talk a little more about false alarms, because they tend to give security systems a bad name. A lot of people who own one will tell you that a full-fledged security system can be a very demanding partner to share your home with. It's demanding because its purpose is to keep "uninvited guests" out of your home. That makes it demanding on the family because, if the system is on, you have to let it know, every time you enter or leave, that you're legitimate, that it's your house and you belong there. Some people come to feel this is a nuisance. They turn the system off and use it only on special occasions, as when they leave on holidays. A large number of burglaries happen in homes armed to the teeth with alarm systems that homeowners simply fail to use on an around-the-clock basis because the systems are not respectful of those who operate them carelessly.

Moreover, you won't always find the local police very enthusiastic about security systems. Electronic devices of all kinds have an often outdated reputation with them for producing false alarms, so that police don't always take them as seriously as they might. Indeed, while some security companies claim to have the false alarm rate in certain cities down as low as 2 percent, our police department told us that "over 90 percent of our security system alerts are false alarms" (albeit mostly from commercial establishments).

Finally, a lot of people are looking for the "perfect" security system, you buy it off the shelf, plug it in, and it works. Well, a good security system must be both well balanced (have the right kind of sensors located in the right places) and well matched to the environment it's intended to protect. Since no two homes or apartments are exactly alike, the closest thing to a "perfect" security system is one that's customized to your particular needs. Luckily, the latest generation of security systems seems to be more "owner-friendly"—a little more able to distinguish between keyholders and intruders entering the house with a crowbar. Nonetheless, if you're going to have a security system, you must use it on a regular basis, understand its limits, and be prepared for the usual (minor) inconveniences that are part of living in an electronically protected environment.

Types of Security Systems

There are, roughly speaking, two kinds of home security systems, based on the kinds of alarms they raise:

Noisemakers rely on you and/or your neighbors to hear an alarm and respond appropriately to the problem. These are available either as individual components or as a package and range from the simple to the complex. Depending where you physically locate this kind of system in the home, the amount of wiring involved, and the need to conceal that wiring, installation can likewise range from the quick and easy to the drawn out and expensive.

Centrally monitored systems sound a local alarm and automatically notify a 24-hour monitoring station, providing security staff with data as to the specific disturbance. The monitoring station, in turn, automatically alerts either your local emergency services or rings a telephone number of your choice. With systems like these, the security service usually supplies everything, either leasing you the equipment and charging you a monthly leasing and monitoring fee, plus installation, or selling you the equipment outright and charging you the installation and monitoring fees only. The monitoring fee generally runs $25 to $35 a month, although a few companies monitor for as little as $15 a month.

These two types of systems easily combine as one, offering dual protection by both scaring off the intruder (with on-site noise) and calling in outside assistance (with an automatic telephone dialer). Other permutations on the two types include on-site noisemakers that come professionally installed or just the opposite—monitored systems that anyone can install by following instructions supplied by the manufacturer. As a general rule, however, centrally monitored "hard-wired" systems most often come professionally installed; simple on-site noisemakers are usually professionally installed if hard-wired and owner-installed if wireless.

Before proceeding with installation, let's break a typical security system down into its basic elements and see what makes it work. Security systems are all made up of the same type of components—the same "basics" and the same "extras." But which are the basics and which are the extras?

Components of a Home Security System

The primary components in every home security system include sensors (detecting devices), a control unit (to regulate the system), and a power siren or horn (to sound the alarm). Broadly speaking, *perimeter sensors* (usually magnetic contacts on windows and doors) are basics, and *area sensors* (motion or radiation detectors that respond to anyone entering a protected interior, such as a hallway) are extras. Both sensor types relay signals that are routed to the basic *console,* or extra *control panel,* either via basic *wires* or small *radio transmitters* (hence "hard-wired" and "wireless"), some of which are basic, others (if you choose to add them) extras. The console or control panel in turn triggers the basic *alarm system* (an on-site noisemaker and/or an extra *automatic telephone dialer,* which alerts the neighborhood, as well as a 24-hour *central monitor*).

Consoles are likewise equipped with extras, including a choice of *operating modes* like "instant" alarm (HOME) and "delayed" alarm (AWAY), giving the user time to enter and exit the premises, and a memory function key (TEST) used for programming the owner's personal access code (PAC). There is also an optional "panic button" (EMERGENCY), located either on the console or on a "remote-entry keypad," or a separate remote control for

172

Table 9.1 Home Security System Inventory

Component	Description	Price
Console	The heart of the system. It operates either off alternating current, battery, or both. Any break in the current flowing through the system causes the alarm to sound.	$200 to $600, depending on make and model
Perimeter sensors (hard-wired, or wireless via radio transmitters)	*Magentic contacts* mounted on door and window frames	$5 to $9
	glass-breakage sensors	$6 to $14
	"wired" window screens	$75 to $100
	foil strips on glass	$1 per foot
Interior sensors:		
Hard-wired or wireless	*Passive infared*—detects body heat in room area	$125 to $160
	Ultrasonic—measures movement via sound wave distortion	$120 to $150
	Microwave—measures movement via radio wave distortion	$100 to $160
	Combination units (any two of the above paired to detect, for example, both heat and sound).	$200 and up
Hard-wired only	*Pressure-sensitive floor mat*—wired mats sound alarm when stepped on	$6 per foot
	Wired window screen—sounds alarm if screen damage occurs	$105 to $120
Transmitters (battery-powered)	Send Radio Frequency (RF) signal if sensor contact is broken.	$25 to $40
Telephone dialer	Automatically dials monitoring station and gives status report.	$120 to $150

signaling an instant alarm from anywhere in the house. The inventory in Table 9.1 will help differentiate the core system from the many options that are available.

As we've indicated, "hard-wired" and "wireless" systems differ in the way the sensor signal reaches the control panel or console. Electrical wires obviously carry the signal in hard-wired systems. In wireless systems, any number of individual transmitters signal a console equipped with a built-in RF receiver. The battery-operated transmitters must be tested regularly to ensure a ready power supply. As a general rule, each set of sensors—one each on doors, windows, panes of glass, and so on—requires its own transmitter, although multiple sensors can be coupled to a single transmitter. For example, if two windows are located side by side, sensors for each window can be attached to a single transmitter located between the two.

That covers the way the building blocks fit together interchangeably to form a composite security system. But before this information can be put to good use in identifying which type of system, if any, to consider looking into, something else that has a strong bearing on the selection process has to be considered: Who should install a security system?

Professional Versus Do-It-Yourself Installation

Just as there are two types of security systems (noisemakers and centrally monitored systems) and two types of installation (hard-wired and transmitter-signaled), so there are two ways to go about installation—professionally or by the owner. A broad understanding of installation options will clear up any confusion regarding home security system as a complete "package," including components and labor, versus a components-only approach, with the owner supplying the necessary labor to complete the installation.

It's more or less standard practice that *hard-wired* centrally monitored systems come with professional installation. That is to say, the choice is made by the supplier to include installation in the price of the product that the consumer purchases. This eliminates a lot of doubt as to who is responsible, not just for the initial hookup but also for the trouble-free operation and maintenance of the system over the long term. Since these systems are under the scrutiny of the security company's monitoring service 24 hours a day, professional installation becomes part and parcel of the systematic protection (prompt response to emergencies) that these systems are intended to provide.

And frankly, with all the highly specialized features available on these systems, you probably wouldn't want it any other way. The manufacturer- or supplier-trained professionals who hook up these systems know how to lick the environmental problems that plague sensitive equipment (air movement, heat sources, vibrations, glass, etc.) and fine-tune features such as self-testing battery devices and dual-detection technology by which the system double-checks itself each time an emergency situation arises. Specialized features like wired window screens should be left to the professional. But since all this costs money (we're coming to how much in a minute), it's important to note there are other cheaper and easier (though not always safer) ways to go.

Hard-wired do-it-yourself installations become a possibility when we switch to the simpler noisemaker system. An owner who is handy can save as much as 40 to 60 percent by installing a hard-wired on-site noisemaker since the bulk of the installation cost in these labor-intensive systems is in running and concealing wire. The move away from central monitoring also opens up the DIY option because this kind of system is no longer tied to a parts and labor "package" but is instead available (minus the monitoring equipment) over the counter on an à la carte basis. So, why the hard-wired approach if it still requires a troublesome degree of skill on the part of the installer?

The home security industry was founded on hard-wired systems, and to this day experts continue to put trust in this type of installation over the more recent radio transmitter technology—and with good reason. Until recently, old-fashioned hard-wired systems were generally more reliable and comparatively free of interference and false alarm problems. Moreover, you don't have to be an electronics genius to install one. Anybody with fair aptitude for technical detail can string wire, install sensors, and tie them into an alarm control device that's reasonably dependable.

We stress "reasonably" dependable because nonprofessional work is most often based on trial and error. Since the problem of false alarms can all too often be traced to owner error—either in day-to-day operation or unskilled, shoddy installation—it may well be worth turning the installation over to a qualified and experienced professional to ensure that the system is functionally sound from the start.

Of course, if you scrap the DIY option, you can then contract the job out to an independent security engineer. This way, as your own contractor, you'll be able to watch the gaps in your security closing with each additional piece of equipment installed and check your security status as you go. In building up a security system in stages, the more components you add, obviously, the more protection you get. Once you've reached the level of protection you feel comfortable with, that's where you stop. This way you don't buy more security than you actually need.

DIY installation finally moves within easy reach of the average security consumer in wireless installations. Recent advances in transmitters and receivers (improved "coded signals") have made radio frequencies and battery power a lot more dependable. In installing wireless equipment, there is a quantum leap between the few minutes it takes to mount a transmitter on each window or door and the hours (or days) involved in running and concealing wire throughout the house—under carpet and behind walls—physically linking each sensor set to the hard-wired control panel. Wireless systems, therefore, are obviously easier and faster and may be cheaper as well if you're faced with paying an electrical contractor several hundred dollars to rough in wiring.

A technical detail about DIY wireless installation: These systems are wireless only to a point. Power sirens must still be hard-wire-connected to the control system. As always, this wire must be carefully concealed because the system will not broadcast a distress signal if this wire is cut or disconnected.

Since the choice between all these variables—monitored or unmonitored, wireless or hard-wired, DIY or professional installation—also involves the cost factor, let's move on to that and compare costs on a couple of typical systems.

How Much Does a Good Security System Cost?

The cost of a security system basically depends on four variable factors:

- The amount of protection called for
- The size and layout of property being protected
- The technology needed to do the job
- Who does the installation

Any one of these can double or halve the price, but to arrive at a ballpark figure of what a security system will cost, there's a convenient rule of thumb often used by security experts:

- The cost of an adequate security system averages about one percent of a home's value.

In other words, a $150,000 home can be "adequately" protected for about $1500, a $75,000 home for about $750. Depending on your shopping list, you certainly can put together some kind of security package within this price

176

guideline. If, however, you're planning to call in a consultant from one of the major manufacturers or installers to do the job, it might be more realistic to raise that guideline another ½ percent, allowing $937 for a $75,000 home and just over $2000 for a $150,000 home.

In mid-1986, the "average" home in the United States cost $84,000, so the "average" security system should come in, according to the rule, at around $840. In time, more and more security suppliers will be able to match that figure, but at the moment it still takes some comparison shopping to stay within the 1 percent guideline. Let's look at some examples.

As the networks of nationwide security services reach out to more and more consumers, central monitoring services are becoming more reliable as well as more affordable. Not too long ago, a clever burglar could bypass such systems by tying up the phone line linking your home to the central monitoring station. The latest telephone dialers now come with built-in incoming call override or "line seizure" devices to keep the line permanently open for emergency use. Some of the more expensive systems also require a direct phone line to be used exclusively for equipment-monitoring purposes. If a break-in or other emergency occurs, the alarm signal is automatically dialed to the monitoring station via this private line.

To get an idea of both what centrally monitored systems do in an emergency situation and what they cost, let's compare a couple of systems—one hard-wired, professionally installed, and leased to the user, the other wireless, purchased outright, and installed by the owner. Both strike a well-measured balance in their respective approaches to home security.

Since the Brink's Home Security System arrived on the market in the early 1980s, it has become the fastest-growing fully monitored service in the country. The company recently introduced a standard home security package that is professionally installed, centrally monitored, and available on a lease basis. Key features of the basic package include three perimeter (door) sensors, a passive infrared area (motion) detector, a power siren, and a wall-mounted console with the usual operating modes (OFF, HOME, AWAY, etc.) as well as separate multiemergency keys for directly alerting police, fire, or medical emergency services with one press of a button. The system also has a backup power supply in case of power failure, individual "zones" for separate control of perimeter and interior areas, automatic reset and self-test capabilities, and a four-digit personal access code with add-on auxiliary codes possible. Finally, to overcome possible false alarms, the Brink's system is equipped with dual-detection technology, requiring not one but a sequence of warning signals to produce a full emergency alert.

As with other similar systems, the Brink's national monitoring center (located in Dallas, Texas) can read the precise nature of the emergency—burglary, fire, or medical alert—from the signal coming from the monitored premises. Within seconds of verifying the emergency with the owner, the monitoring station is in voice contact with the appropriate local emergency service—police, fire department, or medical emergency unit—providing specific information pertaining to the emergency, including hazardous conditions on the premises, medical history of the occupants, and so on.

The cost of the standard Brink's home security package is based on a two-year contract that includes a lifetime warranty on parts and a one-year warranty on labor. An extended labor warranty is available at $60 a year, starting with the second year. As centrally monitored systems go, this one is very affordably priced. There is a one-time $95 connection fee and thereafter a monthly monitoring and leasing charge of $19.50. For a supplementary fee, the package can be expanded to include additional sensors, a smoke sensor, a heat detector, a portable medical emergency pendant, and a separate portable panic button. As it comes, the standard Brink's system is probably adequate for the "average" three-door home with separate front, patio or rear, and garage entrances. How close does it come to the 1 percent cost guideline? Figure that $19.50 per month × 24 months + $95 connection fee = $563 for protection over the initial contract period. The longer the system is leased, the closer it comes to surpassing the 1 percent benchmark. At an ongoing $294 a year ($234 plus a $60 service contract after the first year), it would take just under 2½ years to reach the hypothetical $840 benchmark, during which time you wouldn't have to worry about maintenance or depreciation on a purchased system but after which your long-term outlay would exceed the 1 percent guideline.

Next, let's compare the Brink's leased system with another recent entry into the field of home security. This one is wireless, can be purchased outright, and is easily installed by the buyer. Moreover, it offers central monitoring equipment as an over-the-counter option. With this system, the average home security consumer can purchase and install a complete multiemergency security product without need of professional assistance.

The Keepsafer system is a wireless perimeter system recently introduced by the home security division of the Schlage Lock Company. Its slim console is designed with a microwave look that blends in discretely on a modern kitchen countertop. The basic Keepsafer comes with a programma-

178

ble personal access code, three operational modes plus a panic button, and a starter kit of two transmitter-sensor sets. Without any of the optionals available with it, the Keepsafer lists for $179, with additional sensor-transmitter sets listing at $25 each. For this you get equipment that uses an advanced coded RF signal and a console with zoned modes of operation (allowing instant or delayed alarms on specific doors), plus an emergency panic button that sounds the built-in alarm instantly, even when the console is in the OFF mode, and an automatic alarm shutoff and system reset after five minutes if the alarm is not turned off manually before then.

A more elaborate version of the basic Schlage system is the Keepsafer Plus, which adds a third transmitter-sensor and a portable remote control to the starter kit, along with two more operating modes on the console, an auxiliary alarm for fire or medical alerts, and a daytime advisory tone for signaling the occupants whenever outside doors are used. Among the many additional options available with the Keepsafer Plus are an area sensor (passive infrared), a rechargeable backup battery, glass-break detectors, bedside panic button, medical alarm, smoke monitor, power siren, and no limit on the number of transmitter-sensor sets that can be added.

The main Keepsafer Plus option, however, is an automatic telephone dialer that links the system to Schlage's central monitoring services. Let's say there's a break-in. Here's how it works. Operating in the INSTANT mode, the power alarm goes off, alerting anyone in the home or immediate vicinity. The automatic telephone dialer simultaneously alerts Schlage's central monitoring station via an 800-series WATTS line (no charge to the subscriber). If the homeowner is on the phone, the dialer seizes the line and keep on dialing. On receiving the incoming emergency call, the monitoring station verifies the emergency in the following way. If the owner answers the phone, the emergency is canceled only if the owner uses a "duress" password. (A wrong password is understood to signify that the owner is unable to give the right password—as, for example, when at gunpoint). The central monitoring station then notifies the local police, fire department, or medical emergency services, depending on the nature of the alert. From that point on it's up to the local authorities. (Note: If your local police take more than 10 minutes to reach you on a burglary alert, a centrally monitored system may not be worth the additional cost unless you are using it for fire and medical emergencies as well.)

A unique feature of the Keepsafer system, mentioned earlier but not explained, is the advanced coded RF signal, which is custom-programmed by the individual owner as follows. Each transmitter is equipped with an eight-digit bank of switches. According to how these switches are set, the receiver, likewise equipped with a matching set of switches, receives a coded signal, making the system virtually immune to false alarms. In other words, this digital coding feature reduces or eliminates "random input" from outside RF signals—passing two-way radios, a neighbor's garage-door opener, or another nearby security system—that otherwise might trigger an alarm. These coding switches, moreover, are used to "zone" the interior by enabling exterior doors to be set on either DELAYED or INSTANT response and glass, smoke, and area detectors to be set on the INSTANT only mode. Finally, a three-digit personal access code, also programmed by the owner, enables only those who know the code to access or disable the system. A special feature for preschool-age children is a single-digit PAC that automatically repeats a one-digit instruction in triplicate, enabling the junior user to access the console with the touch of a single key.

The Keepsafer Plus starter set lists for $349, to which a full range of options can be added, among them the telephone dialer, $120; Schlage's monthly monitoring fee, $15; the passive area detector, $126; smoke alarm, about $90; backup battery, about $20; power siren, about $20; and additional remote control units, about $65. The grand total for all this (less the monitoring fee and the extra remote unit) comes to about $725, noticeably under the rule-of-thumb guideline of $840 and for a system of well above average quality.

We have the Keepsafer Plus system, and although it's fairly new, we feel that we can recommend it. We installed it ourselves, needing only the screwdriver on our trusty Swiss army knife to do the job. The only slight difficulties we encountered were in adjusting the sensitivity of the glass-break detectors so that we could tell if they were working or not (who wants to break the glass to find out?) and mounting the sensor-transmitter sets on antique doors and door facings in our turn-of-the-century home—a problem clearly related to period architecture (no flush surfaces) and not to twentieth-century security devices.

As the technology continues to improve with each new wave of products, the trend in coming years will probably increasingly be toward owner-installed systems such as these. Other similar systems currently available (but without the advanced coded-signal technology) include the Amway Corporation's wireless Amguard Perimeter Alarm, an owner-installed on-site noise-maker with central monitoring as an optional feature. The Amguard II starter set consists of a console with four different alarm signals, two transmitters, and a remote control for $795. Important add-ons are à la carte, including the telephone dialer ($150) and monitoring service ($15 a month). The Amway five-year warranty is about the best in the business. Other systems are the Perm-A-Tron ($229.99 basic, $299.00 deluxe) and the Lifesaver VI, made by Tyrnetics, Inc. (basic $89.95 with one transmitter-sensor set; $189.50 for four transmitter sets and a power siren).

Additional Operating Costs

There are often unexpected operating costs that you'll need to factor into the overall expense of running a home security system. Most municipalities charge an annual $10 to $20 *license fee,* with a penalty for false alarms. Typically you can expect the license to be withdrawn after three false alarms. The reason for this is that it costs the average city an estimated $700 to $800 every time the police and fire departments are called out on an alarm. The license fee may be higher if the security system includes a panic button. Why more for this extra security feature? Perhaps too many people push panic buttons before stopping to consider the cost to the community.

Another operating cost is that security systems have to be properly maintained. To qualify for an ongoing insurance discount, for example, an inspection of your system is required every three years. So just make sure that you have a good warranty to start with and that you spend whatever else it takes to keep your system in good working order.

A minor ongoing expense with wireless systems is battery replacement. Since the system is entirely battery-dependent, this isn't an area you'll want to try to save money on. Batteries should be tested every few months and replaced regularly twice a year.

The overriding point here is that protection, if you need it, isn't something you should skimp on. Yet there's no reason why home security can't be both cost-conscious and adequate.

Keeping It Safe but Simple

Burglary is a "crime of opportunity." A good home security system is probably the most effective way of reducing that opportunity. Chances are you'll force a burglar to move on in search of easier quarry if he has to double-check before entering premises that are equipped with electronic home surveillance devices. If you're ready to take the plunge into electronic home protection, the following check list of questions should be useful in your shopping. It applies to all kinds of systems—monitored, hard-wired, and wireless.

- Is the system centrally monitored and, if so, is the monitoring station approved by Underwriters' Laboratories? (Note: Wireless systems are not subject to U.L. standards.)
- Does the system include any "interior detection devices" (in addition to the usual "perimeter" protection of doors and windows)?
- Is the system zoned and, if so, how many zones does it have?
- Does the central station receive status reports at regular intervals concerning the condition of your system?
- What kind of warranty comes with the equipment?
- Is the control panel or console easily reached, or do you use a remote control for arming and disarming the system?
- Is there a delayed alarm, giving you time to arm and disarm the system when you exit or enter the premises?
- Is there a detachable, external power siren?
- Are there test lights on all batteries?
- Are there a self-silencing device and an automatic reset once the system has been alerted?
- Does an indicator light warn you that the system has been activated or tampered with in your absence?
- Is the panic button located on a fixed keypad, or can it be sounded from anywhere in the house by a portable remote control?
- Does the security company provide references, and are employees who make house calls bonded?

(Why bonded? Police files are full of reports of burglars "casing" houses while posing as security agents. One house in our neighborhood was burglarized the day after a highly reputable system was installed. When the homeowner reported the break-in, the security company was quick to point out that their product was aimed at avoidance, but not prevention, of housebreaking. On close inspection, however, it was apparent that the system had been sabotaged by someone who knew the exact location of the disabling devices. Although the homeowner's warranty only covered equipment failure, the security company agreed, in the interest of good public relations, to replace the system and look into the matter further.)

Just remember, if you do get a home security system, keep up your routine precautions as well. Don't trust all your protection to the security system alone, no matter how good it is. Next, use your security. Don't get caught with your protection switched off when you need it most. And for your own safety, never confront an intruder (or allow anyone else in your family to do so) in response to an alarm. Instead, notify the police. They alone have the training and experience to respond to home security emergencies.

Something else to watch for: A new product directly linking home insurance to home security. Introduced in California in the Spring of 1987 by IDS, a Minneapolis-based subsidiary of American Express Financial Services, and Brink's Home Security, Inc., Protection 24 offers a standard homeowner's insurance policy backed by electronic security. Although a price base has yet to be established nationwide, IDS-Brink's is expected to price the new product aggressively. We think the insurance/security combination is the wave of the future, and that Protection 24 is something to keep an eye on.

A few testimonials illustrate what some other people we know have done to protect their homes and their families. A couple, close personal friends, were in doubt about whether or not to include a security system in a new home they were building. It was still early enough in the project to string wire under floors and inside open walls, but it wasn't in the budget to do so, much less think about the price tag on the rest of the system while trying to contain the runaway costs on the building itself. The building contractor wanted $600 to lay in the wiring alone, and, to make matters worse, our friends were under the impression that burglars could easily defeat a perimeter system anyhow by "plugging" the magnetic sensors with a spare metal contact when opening windows and doors. We explained that once the contact was broken, even if just for a second, an alarm signal would have been transmitted to the control panel—an irreversible event in the better systems. Without trying to sell our friends on the idea of electronic protection, we pointed out that by stringing the wire now, they would have the option at a later date of adding the trimmings. Even if they never put in the system, their property value would increase due to the house's being "system-ready." In the end, we showed them how to zone the interior of the house, helped them pick a place for a control panel, and string wire from window one in zone A to the panel location. In the end, they finished the wiring themselves for just under $30—the price of a reel of U.L.-approved wire (or one wireless transmitter).

In this regard, the difference between working with existing structures and dwellings under construction is enormous. It's far easier and less expensive to "rough in" wiring for a security system before the walls and floors go in. For only few dollars you can, like our friends, hard-wire every window and door in the house.

Other neighbors, having lost several microwave ovens, stereos, and television sets in the course of numerous break-ins, finally installed a fancy brand-name system. They report that over and above having not been bothered again (and the 5 percent discount they're now getting on their home insurance), the real saving is in "being able to come home and know, thanks to the cheerful beeping tone that greets you, that the place is just like you left it."

Summary

According to an FBI report released in mid-1986, crimes against the American home are on the decline. Based on that encouraging news, it's probably safe to assume that the current security system boom in the consumer market must be having a positive effect on home crime prevention. If you think you'd feel more secure with an electronic protection system, let's review a few basic points to keep in mind:

- Home security systems range from over-the-counter products that anyone can purchase and install to complex leased systems installed and maintained (and monitored) by professional security agencies.
- Monitored systems are watched over by professional security services that contact your local emergency services in the event of fire, burglary, or medical emergency.
- Any kind of sensing device, including a smoke detector, can be connected to an automatic telephone dialer and report alarms to the number of your choice. It doesn't have to be part of a security system to do this. But bear in mind that most communities will not permit privately owned monitoring equipment to be connected directly to local emergency services. For that you must go through a professional agency.
- As a rough estimate, expect to pay about 1 percent of the value of your home or apartment for a security system that will offer adequate protection.

- To be effective, a burglar alarm must be used consistently. Studies show that many homes equipped with alarms are still often unprotected because people fail to turn them on. So if you have a security system, make good use of it.
- Like any protection device, a burglar alarm will deter, but not necessarily prevent, a burglar from breaking into your home. Trust your possessions to a home security system, but not your life.

III

Legal Protection

10

Writing a Will

SEVEN AMERICANS OUT OF TEN DIE WITHOUT A WILL, AND NINE OUT OF TEN DIE WITHOUT NAMING A GUARDIAN FOR THEIR CHILDREN.

IF YOU DIE WITHOUT A WILL, YOUR SPOUSE (CONTRARY TO COMMON ASSUMPTION) DOES NOT "AUTOMATICALLY GET EVERYTHING." YOUR LACK OF PLANNING WILL COST YOUR HEIRS TIME, MONEY, AND EMOTIONAL DISTRESS.

Why Every Adult Needs a Will

A will is a legal document that directs the distribution of your property after your death. The need for a well-written will is universal—do not make the mistake of assuming that your estate is too small to require one. In fact, there are four basic reasons why every adult, male or female, young or old, employed or not, with or without dependents, should have a valid will.

1. *To set forth the disposition of your property.* If you do not have a will, your property will be distributed according to inflexible formulas determined by the laws of the state in which you reside. Most people assume that a

surviving spouse automatically inherits everything if the other spouse dies and is free to use those assets as seen fit. Not true! Depending on the law of your state, a surviving spouse may be entitled to only one-half or one-third of your estate or to a share equal to a child's share, so that what he or she gets depends on the number of children. Moreover, the surviving spouse would be restricted in the use of the minor children's inheritance.

In other words, the remaining parent is not necessarily free to use the children's funds in the way he or she thinks best to provide for them. Usually, the court is required to name a guardian for the child's property. The remaining parent, though usually the first choice, is still obliged to contend with the legal formalities and expenses of court-appointed guardianship. All this makes for unnecessary hardship on surviving family members, *especially* if the estate is small.

2. *To choose a guardian for your children and other dependents.* In the absence of a will, a court will decide who will raise your children in the event both parents die. If you don't name a guardian, your estate will have to pay a bond and fees for a court-appointed guardian. In addition, most state laws require a court-appointed guardian to make an annual accounting to the court, which adds yet more cost and fees, which will be paid out of your estate.

And the process of selecting a guardian is often very emotional. By naming a guardian you will avoid fights among family members over who should take care of your children. Moreover, if you don't have a will, in most states the court will also appoint a guardian for the *assets* that go to the children, even if one parent is still living. Again, this drains funds from the estate and entails legal formalities and court time.

3. *To avoid court involvement in probate proceedings.* In most states, you're permitted to "self-prove" your will, meaning that you can appoint an *independent* executor who will make sure your estate is distributed according to your wishes with almost no court involvement in any probate proceedings. In contrast, if you die without a will—called "intestate"—the court will appoint an *administrator* to handle the executor's tasks, who will charge *fees* against the estate for doing so. These are sometimes very stiff and can take a disproportionate bite out of a small estate. Court administrators must also be *bonded* in most states, and this results in additional expense. Instead, you should write a will and consider appointing as executor your spouse or a friend who will probably waive an executor's fee. (We'll talk about the qualifications of a good executor shortly.) Thus by writing a will and naming an

190

independent executor to handle your estate, you win twice—first by not having the court appoint an administrator who will charge your estate fees to distribute your assets, and second by avoiding court involvement in probate proceedings.

4. *To minimize the tax burden on your estate.* For medium-sized and larger estates, considerable money may be saved by writing a will that incorporates a legal device called a *testamentary trust.* A trust is an arrangement whereby you give assets to a trustee to manage and invest for the benefit of the trust's beneficiaries. There are several tax and nontax reasons for creating such a trust in your will. Property given to your minor children through a testamentary trust is generally not subject to estate tax until the death of the children. Trusts are also useful in the instance when your children are young or your other dependents are financially inexperienced, as the trustee will manage and invest the trust property for your children or dependents.

In addition to using a testamentary trust, a well-drawn will allows you to take advantage of tax law provisions such as the marital deduction and the unified tax credit.

The *marital deduction* lets you give an unlimited amount of property to your spouse tax-free. That is, with this deduction you defer paying any taxes on your estate until the death of the surviving spouse. Using the marital deduction, you can give the remainder of your estate *outright* to your spouse, giving your spouse full control over the property at your death. Or you can put the remainder of your estate *in trust* for the sole benefit of your spouse during his or her lifetime but direct that the trust assets go to your children or another individual upon the death of your spouse. This second device is a means to ensure that any assets remaining in your estate after your spouse's death will pass to whomever you choose.

The *unified credit* allows you to give property worth up to $600,000 to *anyone* without having to pay any estate tax. As long as this property is given *in trust* for the benefit of your spouse and children or is simply given outright to someone other than your spouse, the property will avoid taxation at your death as well as at that beneficiary's death. Since the unified credit allows you to name *anyone* as the beneficiary for up to $600,000 of property value without paying estate tax, it is obviously a useful device for someone who is not married or who is married but for some reason doesn't want to use the marital deduction.

To be honest, anyone reading these words who doesn't yet have a will should not let another week pass without taking steps to get one drawn up.

Take the case of Stephen and Shelly to heart. They married right out of high school and had a baby shortly thereafter. They were young and healthy and gave no thought to wills. Besides, they didn't believe they had enough in the way of assets to need a will. A few years passed, they bought a house, Stephen got a good job, and his father died and left him and his brothers a house, which they sold at a good price. Stephen's share of the proceeds was intended for his little girl's college education. Then tragedy struck: Stephen was killed in a freak accident in an electrical storm. Contrary to what most people would assume, Shelly—or for that matter, Shelly and the baby—did not inherit all of Stephen's assets. Because he died intestate, they were divided according to state law—by which a sizable chunk of his estate was awarded to his surviving brothers! The court also appointed an independent executor who charged fees against the state, when Shelly would have been able to handle the job. Moreover, the estate was tied up in court for more than two years. And even now that it's finally cleared, Shelly is still required to make annual trips to court to account for how she is spending the assets that did go to their daughter.

Do You Need a Lawyer in Writing a Will?

Yes, you probably do. Forget the hastily scrawled, "I, Jane Doe, being of sound mind and body . . ." approach. Some states will not allow a handwritten (called "holographic") will under any circumstances. Others may allow them as long as they observe certain legal formalities, formalities most of us wouldn't know about. For example, would you have known that most states require *three* witnesses to the signing of a will, and none of them may be beneficiaries, lest they risk invalidating the will or disinheriting themselves? The point is that a will must be clear and unambiguous in the eyes of the court. Unfortunately, a will written in everyday language that is perfectly clear to a lay reader may in fact be full of legal loopholes and ambiguities.

What about "fill-in-the-blank" wills, standard forms that you can complete and get notarized and witnessed? These are available for a few dollars in some stationery stores or from life insurance agents. However, these are recommended against for the same reasons cited for holographic wills. Wills and estate planning are a complicated business; they cry out for personalized, professional attention. That means an attorney specializing in estate planning. Particularly if you have a larger estate, not just any lawyer will do. Changing tax laws are too complex, there are too many formalities to be observed, and the potential cost of mistakes is too high. You should have an estate lawyer from the state where you legally reside, pay taxes, and would expect your will to be probated. This is because state laws have a lot to say about the final disposition of your property, and they differ significantly.

The cost of hiring a lawyer will obviously vary, depending on how complex your estate is. A simple, basic will can cost as little as $50 to $150—more in big cities, where the lawyer's cost of doing business is high. For a larger estate, a more complicated will that sets up trusts and related provisions can cost very substantially more. However, if your estate is large, it's virtually certain that an estate lawyer will save you more than you'll pay the lawyer in fees by drawing up a "tax-sensitive" will. Be sure to discuss fees with the lawyer in advance of doing business. Comparison shopping is, as always, a good idea.

If you cannot afford a private lawyer, there are legal clinics that can help. They can do an adequate job for you and may charge fees of less than $50 for a simple will based on a standard form.

Will Maker's Checklist

To save your attorney time and you money, draw up in advance a comprehensive list of information about your personal affairs and assets and liabilities that the attorney needs to draw up the will. Include everything on this checklist:

Personal Information

- Names, addresses, dates of birth of you, your spouse, children, and other immediate family members
- Location of birth certificates
- Social Security numbers and location of cards
- Date and place of marriage and location of marriage certificate; information on any prenuptial agreement
- Military service branch, dates of service and discharge; location of discharge papers
- Names and addresses of guardian(s) for minor children in the event of the death of both parents
- If previously married, date and place, and name of former spouse; location of his or her death certificate, or date, place, and location

of divorce papers. If divorced, note if contested and, if so, who brought the action. Was there a divorce settlement or antenuptial agreement? (This information will help the lawyer determine if the spouse retains any inheritance rights.)

- Any immediate relatives (especially children) who are handicapped or require special care
- Name(s) and address(es) of the person or institution you want named as the trustee(s) and executor(s) of your estate
- If you own a second residence, its address and the amount of time you spend there; note where you vote and pay income taxes.
- Location of copies of income tax returns, and name and address of preparer
- Name and addresses of accountant and stockbroker; name of any person to whom you have given power of attorney
- Names and addresses of your employers and location of your employment contracts, if you have such
- Funeral arrangements preferred

Assets and Liabilities

- Details of savings and checking accounts, including bank location, account numbers, location of passbook
- Details of life insurance policies—insuring company, policy numbers, kind, face amount, location of contract, beneficiaries, name and address of your agent
- Policies owned by others for which you are a beneficiary
- Details of any pension or annuity plan you are entitled to
- Details of stock option or stock purchase plans in which you are enrolled and any other employee benefits that may be payable at your death
- Information on any trust for which you are a beneficiary
- Details of stock and bond accounts
- Details on annuity plans, IRA, Keogh plans, and/or deferred-compensation plans
- Details of any business interest you own; any debts owed to you
- Full itemization of any real estate you own—location, price paid, estimate of current market value, whether ownership is joint, loca-

tion of deeds; any other assets valued at over $200—cars, art, furniture, jewelry, furs, etc.; details of your mortgage debt—institution's name and address, amount owed, term, relevant documents and records. Note if you have mortgage insurance that automatically pays off the mortgage in the event of your death.

- Location of safe-deposit box and key
- Statement of current income
- Details of debts you owe, such as car loans, significant credit card and bank loans, and lease obligations, to whom, and under what terms.

Make extra copies of this checklist and give them to your executor and beneficiaries, as well as to your estate attorney.

Assets That Pass Outside the Will

Assets that are *jointly owned*—as when husband and wife jointly own their home or a bank account—and assets for which a specific *beneficiary* has been named—such as a life insurance policy—are assets that cannot be willed. These are said to "pass outside the will," because they go directly to the beneficiaries. (They are also protected from any creditor's claims.) Other common examples of beneficiary-designated assets that pass outside the will are pension and annuity benefits that continue in some form after your death and U.S. Savings Bonds. Despite the fact that such assets pass outside the estate, your attorney must be informed of them for estate-planning purposes. For example, planning can prevent these assets from being added to your gross estate for the purpose of calculating tax against it. This is an area in which literally tens of thousands of dollars can potentially be saved for the estate by virtue of professional planning!

Selecting Your Executor, Trustee, and Guardian

As we said earlier, if your will provides for an *independent executor,* your estate can be administered largely free from court control, thereby saving a great deal of time and money. The independent executor oversees the procedures involved in the administration of the estate, such as collecting all your assets, paying your debts, and distributing your assets in accordance with the terms of your will. Although the independent executor will often work closely with an attorney, it is important that the independent executor have the judgment, experience, and ability necessary to perform the duties and make the decisions necessary to the administration of your estate. Generally, the spouse is appointed as the initial independent executor, followed by two or three successor executors to ensure that one of them will be able and willing to act as executor when the time comes to probate your will.

The role of the executor clearly entails considerable responsibility and effort. For this effort, the executor is normally paid a commission fixed by state statute or determined by the court on the basis of the complexity of the estate. A surviving spouse or close friend named as executor frequently waives the fee. And for reasons of cost, individuals, rather than banks, are usually appointed as executors. However, we do suggest appointing a bank or trust company as an *alternate* independent executor to ensure that there will always be an independent executor available for the probate of your estate. You may also appoint two equal executors (coexecutors, either two people or an individual and a bank, acting together) to administer the estate, although the use of coexecutors can cause delays and additional paperwork.

Although a nonresident of your state can act as executor (as long as additional steps are taken), experience has shown that this is often unsatisfactory, because an individual residing some distance away is generally unable to satisfy the details of administering an estate as well as a local executor.

If your will sets up a trust of any kind, you'll need to appoint a *trustee*. Whom you should choose as trustee depends in large part on what you want the trustee actually to do. If you want a trustee simply to disburse income generated by the trust's assets to your beneficiaries, that's fairly easy and doesn't require especially developed financial acumen. However, if you want a trustee actually to manage the assets or provide financial advice and supervision to your children, that's another matter. You may have an immediate friend or family member with the qualifications to handle financial details of this kind, but if not, you'll want to consider appointing an attorney (not, however, the one who did your estate plan—there's too much potential for finagling), an accountant or financial planner, a bank, or a trust company as trustee.

Banks and trust companies have the advantage of being staffed to do the required tax accounting and other paperwork. Another common arrangement is to name an individual, usually a family member or close friend, as

196

cotrustee to manage specific investments and disbursements, along with an institution to handle routine investments, accounting, tax reporting, and other paperwork. Note that a beneficiary of a trust should not be named as trustee unless a cotrustee is also named.

Consider the possibilities for conflict of interest as you choose a trustee. An individual, for example, who might later be a beneficiary of the trust might be reluctant to disburse some of the trust's funds in the near term. Your stockbroker might not be a good choice to manage trust securities, as he or she might be tempted to turn over trust stocks in order to earn commissions.

As to trustee costs, they can range from nil to thousands of dollars. Individual trustees (like executors) often waive fees. An institutional trustee will of course have to be paid, so it may be uneconomical to name a bank for a small trust.

Most institutions have a minimum fee, generally ranging from $500 a year to $2500. (Banks may reduce their minimums if the trust's assets are invested in the banks' common trust funds, which are internal mutual funds set up for that purpose). From the minimum, institutional fees for trust management are generally calculated as a percentage of the principal, a percentage of annual income earned by the trust (usually from 4 to 7 percent), or a combination of the two. Be sure to ask if there are extra costs for jobs like preparing tax returns on the trust.

Note that for large trusts, fees are usually negotiable. Again, it pays to comparison-shop. As part of reaching an agreement, always get your trustee fee arrangement in writing.

Finally, in naming *guardians* for your children in your will, carefully consider their age and personal health, their family situation and the impact of the added responsibility your children would bring to that family, and, of course, their personal qualities—their ability and willingness to exert the kind of parental influence you want your children to receive. You must consider as well the potential guardian's financial situation. Although your children will bring with them an inheritance, it may not be enough to cover all the costs of raising and educating them. You must also decide if you want the guardian to be guardian of both the children and the children's assets. If you've set up a trust for the children, it would be a good idea to name a bank or other institution as guardian of the assets, if the children's guardian is financially inexperienced. Finally, you should note in your will if you would like the guardian to adopt the children legally.

Of course, you should discuss the situation thoroughly with any individual you are considering naming as executor, trustee, or guardian. These are not tasks you should surprise someone with after the fact!

Periodic Review of Your Will

Once you have a will, you cannot, unfortunately, lock it in a safe-deposit box and forget about it. For one thing, your safe-deposit box is likely to be sealed by the court at your death, making it a poor place to keep your will. Instead, leave it with your attorney or institutional executor, and keep a copy in a safe place at home that your beneficiaries know about.

But even more important, your will can't just be put away and forgotten because it requires periodic review. Even though a well-drawn will has some built-in flexibility—for example, wording allowing for the birth of a second child—it's essentially a precise document reflecting a given situation. (That's as it should be. Ambiguous wording may result in a will that has to be interpreted by a court, and there's no guarantee that the court will interpret it as you intended.) Of course, a person's situation can change significantly. When it does, the will should be reviewed and updated to reflect all changes.

An appropriate time to review your will is at the birth of a child (even if you think it's written to cover that), at the death of a spouse, if you divorce, if your former spouse remarries, or if you have a significant change—for better or for worse—in your property or income. (For example, if you suffered a significant financial reverse, you might want to eliminate a previously made special bequest to your alma mater to focus the remaining assets on your family. Conversely, if your assets increase substantially, you may need to bring in a professional cotrustee to manage them.) You might also want to review your will if your beneficiaries have a significant change in their financial situation. You should review your will if you move to another state, in case legal formalities differ there. Review it as tax laws change, or if your executor, trustee, or guardian dies or is no longer able or appropriate to serve.

Following the chapter summary we have included a sample will for a married person with one or more children. It contains a testamentary trust, defined earlier. Of course, you should consult an attorney specializing in wills and estate law prior to making your will.

Summary

- Every adult, young or old, male or female, married or not, rich or poor, needs a will. Dying without a will causes unnecessary delay and expense in the disposition of your assets, may result in a higher tax burden on the estate, and causes the court to be excessively involved in these proceedings.
- The more complicated your estate, whether due to the amount or kinds of assets and liabilities or the way you want them disposed, the more important it is to have an estate lawyer's help. The sample will provided at the end of this chapter is a good model but in no way substitutes for the detailed, personal attention of an estate lawyer.
- Consider carefully whom you should appoint as the trustee and executor of your will and the guardian for any dependents. Good executors and trustees have some financial expertise and are able to handle administrative details and paperwork. It's not always best to try to save money on executor and trustee fees by appointing a spouse or close friend to the task.

LAST WILL AND TESTAMENT
OF

_____
(TESTATOR)

THE STATE OF_____
COUNTY OF_____   §   KNOW ALL MEN
                              §   BY THESE PRES-
                                      ENTS

I, (Name of Testator), a resident of (State), do hereby make and publish this, my Last Will and Testament, hereby revoking all Wills and other Testamentary instruments heretofore made by me.

ARTICLE I

I, (Name of Testator), am married and my (Wife or Husband) name is (Name of Spouse). All references in this Will to "my (Wife or Husband)" are to this person. I have (number) child(ren) at this time, whose names are (name of children) and for all purposes under this Will all references hereunder to "my children" shall be deemed to include the above-named children and other children hereafter born to or legally adopted by me. For all purposes under this Will, the word "issue" shall mean children and all direct lineal descendants, including those who are adopted.

ARTICLE II

I direct that all taxes, including interest and penalties thereon, which may be payable by reason of my death, and all of my debts, funeral expenses, and administration expenses shall be charged against and paid out of my residuary estate. No contribution for any of the above taxes upon the proceeds of any insurance policy on my life shall be made by the beneficiary (other than my estate) of any such insurance policy. My executor is given the right to renew and extend, in any form that he deems best, any debt or charge existing at the time of my death.

ARTICLE III

I give, devise, and bequeath unto my (Wife or Husband) all of my remaining estate of every kind and character, real, personal, and mixed, if (Wife or Husband) survives me by thirty (30) days.

ARTICLE IV

If my (Wife or Husband) does not survive me by at least thirty (30) days, I give, devise, and bequeath all of my remaining estate unto (Name of Trustee), Trustee, IN TRUST, for the following uses and purposes, and subject to the following provisions, conditions, and limitations:

(a) *Distributions During the Term of the Trust.*
The Trustee shall distribute unto my living children so much of the income and corpus as my Trustee in his sole discretion shall deem necessary and appropriate to provide for my children's health, education, maintenance, and support. Any income not distributed shall be added to the corpus. Any distributions made under this paragraph need not be equal among beneficiaries and shall not be charged against their respective shares of the Trust.

(b) *Termination and Final Distribution.*
Upon the attainment of the age of twenty-one (21) years by the youngest of my children then living, or if earlier upon the death of the last of my children then under such age, the Trust shall terminate and the Trust corpus and any undistributed income shall be distributed in fee simple and free of trust, unto my children then living.

(c) *Spendthrift Clause.*
No beneficiary of the Trust shall have the right or power to anticipate by assignment or otherwise any income or corpus given to such beneficiary by this Will, nor in advance of actually receiving the same have the right or

power to sell, transfer, encumber, or in any way charge the same; nor shall income or corpus, or any portion of the same, be subject to any execution, garnishment, attachment, insolvency, bankruptcy, or legal proceeding of any character, or legal sequestration, levy or sale, or in any event or manner be applicable or subject, voluntarily or involuntarily, to the payment of such beneficiary's debts.

ARTICLE V

The Trustee of the Trust hereinabove provided for, and his successor(s), if any, shall have and exercise the rights, powers, and privileges provided by the laws of the State of _____ where said duties, provisions, conditions, and limitations are not specified herein.

ARTICLE VI

Should the Trustee named in Article IV above be deceased, unqualified, unable, or unwilling to serve as Trustee, I name (Name of Substitute Trustee) as alternate Trustee under the foregoing Trust.

ARTICLE VII

The Trustee need not post any bond for so acting.

ARTICLE VIII

I appoint my (Wife or Husband) as the Independent (Executrix or Executor) of this Will. If for any reason my (Wife or Husband) is unable or unwilling to act or to continue to act in that capacity, then I appoint (Name of Substitute Independent Executor) as my Independent Executor. I direct that no action shall be taken in any court in the administration of my estate other than the probating and recording of this Will and the return of an inventory, appraisement, and list of claims of my estate. My Independent Executor, whether original, substitute, or successor, is herein referred to as my Executor. No bond or other security shall be required of any Executor appointed under this Will. Any Executor appointed under this Will shall have all those powers given by law.

ARTICLE IX

If my (Wife or Husband) does not survive me by at least thirty (30) days, I name and appoint (Name of Substitute Guardian) as the guardian of the person and estate of each of my minor children. Such guardian shall serve without bond.

ARTICLE X

If my (Wife or Husband) shall die simultaneously with me or if there is no direct evidence to establish that my (Wife or Husband) and I died other than simultaneously, I direct that my (Wife or Husband) be deemed to have predeceased me notwithstanding any provision of law to the contrary and that the provisions of my Will shall be construed on such presumption. If any legatee, devisee, or beneficiary of any trust other than my (Wife or Husband) shall die simultaneously with me or if there is no direct evidence to establish that such person and I died other than simultaneously, I hereby declare that I shall be deemed to have survived such person.

ARTICLE XI

If any part, clause, provision, or condition of this Will is held to be void, invalid, or inoperative, such voidness, invalidity, or inoperativeness shall not affect any other clause, provision, or condition hereof; but the remainder of this Will shall be effective as though such clause, provision, or condition had not been contained herein.

This I make and publish as my Last Will and Testament, hereunto subscribing my name in the presence of

_____,

_____, and

_____, who

have, at my request, and in my presence, and in the presence of each other, also subscribed their names hereto as attesting witnesses, on this _____day of _____, 19___.

This instrument, each preceding page of which is identified by (Name of Testator)'s signature, was subscribed, published, and declared by him to be his Last Will and Testament in our presence, and we, in his presence, at his request, and in the presence of each other hereunto subscribe our names as witnesses, and we declare that at the execution hereof (Name of Testator) was of sound mind and memory and under no constraint.

Witnesses   Residing at:

_____   _____

_____   _____

_____   _____

Self-proving Affidavit

THE STATE OF_____   §
COUNTY OF_____   §
                            §

Before me, the undersigned authority, on this date personally appeared (Name of Testator) and _____, _____, and _____, known to me to be the testator and the witnesses, respectively, whose names are subscribed to the annexed or foregoing instrument in their respective capacities, and all of said persons being by me duly sworn, the said testator declared to me and to the witnesses in my presence that said instrument is his Last Will and Testament and that he had willingly made and executed it as his free act and deed for the purposes expressed therein; and the said witnesses, each on his oath stated to me, in the presence and in the hearing of the testator, that the said testator had declared to them that said instrument is his Last Will and Testament and that he executed the same as such and wanted each of them to sign it as a witness; and upon their oaths each witness stated further that he did sign the same as a witness in the presence of the testator and at his request; that he was at that time eighteen (18) years of age or over and was of sound mind; and that each of said witnesses was then at least eighteen (18) years of age.

                                       _____

                                       Testator

                                       _____

                                       Witness

                                       _____

                                       Witness

                                       _____

                                       Witness

Epilogue

So you see, total coverage isn't really so difficult to tackle. If some topics we've taken on seemed daunting at first, we hope we've showed that by understanding the basics and going at things one step at a time you can become as "expert" as need be in order to protect yourself, your family, and your possessions. And that includes protecting yourself as a consumer as well. There's certainly no need to put blind faith in any kind of insurance or security salesperson. Once you're equipped with all the basic information, you're really the one best qualified to assess your own vital needs.

Nor do you need to buy the most expensive insurance policies or security systems in order to be assured of total coverage. In fact, even a small amount of comparison shopping in these areas can save you *thousands* of dollars. An extravagant claim? Not at all, when you consider that Americans spend on average 11 percent of their disposable income on various insurances alone. With that kind of money at stake, you owe it to yourself to do the homework we've outlined for you in these pages. In this respect we hope Total Coverage has helped and is already repaying your efforts.

Here are some final reminders:

Insurance

- Be sure to read your insurance policies. Take advantage of the ten-day "free look" on policies that many states mandate, during which you can change your mind at no cost to you. Understand the basic terms of policies—deductibles, exclusions, inclusions (many of us don't file claims for reimbursement that is actually due us under the policy's terms), limitations, waiting periods, and so on.

- Know your rights under your various policies. This includes such things as the grace period you have if you miss a payment deadline, the statute of limitations on claims, your right not to accept a settlement you think is unfair, how to and to whom you should file a complaint, and whether the policy is noncancelable and guaranteed renewable.

- Buy insurance for the bigger losses and self-insure for the smaller ones to save money. This generally means taking the largest deductible on your policies that you can reasonably manage. By picking up the cost of the $200 scratch on your car or absorbing the $300 loss of your stereo by theft or waiting 90 days before disability benefits are paid to you, you'll likely save a minimum of 20 percent overall on your insurance premiums.

- Don't buy insurance you don't need. Most "specialty" insurance— cancer insurance, flight and rental car insurance, contact lens insurance, and so on—are usually bad consumer buys. Don't buy excessive amounts of basic coverages, and be careful not to insure the wrong people or things. For example, your goal with life insurance shouldn't be to make your heirs rich (it will certainly make you poor). They should be expected to use the life insurance principal, not live off the interest. And many three- or four-year-old cars don't warrant comprehensive or collision coverage. Children don't need life insurance at all. And so on.

- Coordinate your coverage to the extent possible. Many agents— and, more important, companies—offer several or even all of the basic coverages. The package approach will generally result in a lower overall insurance bill than separate coverages. The larger companies like Aetna, the Travelers, Allstate, Kemper, Liberty Mutual, Metropolitan, and Prudential generally offer health, life, disability, home, and auto insurance. The savings can be significant— 20 percent or more—but will vary by company, once again illustrating the importance of comparison shopping.

- Always look for and ask about discounts on any policy you are considering or perhaps already have. Widely available discounts in life insurance (for example, for nonsmokers), for homeowner's insurance (security devices), for car insurance (certified defensive drivers, seniors) are listed throughout the text.

- Reassess your insurance coverage annually and whenever you experience a significant change in your life—if you marry or divorce, at the birth of a child or the death of a spouse, if you move (especially out of state), if you suffer a financial setback or reap a windfall. Here we're concerned not just in keeping pace with inflation but with your changing personal needs.
- Keep all your insurance papers in a safe, fireproof place *other than* a safe-deposit box (which is usually sealed at your death for a time); file duplicates with your insurance agent(s) and with your attorney.

Security

- Personal security is, to an important degree, a matter of attitude. If you think and behave as if it can only happen to the other guy, you've made yourself more vulnerable than would otherwise be the case. We're not advocating a paranoid or "ready for action" mentality, just general alertness to potential problems and a prudent approach to coping with them. Alertness and prudence, as a matter of attitude, are your best self-protection.
- Before getting carried away, get basic. Before signing up for a karate course, set safety standards and practice basic preventive measures. Before stopping a burglar, stop a fire (from the loss standpoint, one fire equals a thousand burglaries). Before spending a lot of money on an electronic security system, install basic high-security hardware and security lighting fixtures around your home.
- The correct response to a fire or burglar alarm or a medical emergency is to phone 911, the emergency number. Police, firefighting, and medical crews are trained and equipped to deal with such emergencies, whereas the homeowner or person on the street is not. An exception to this rule is CPR, which everyone should know how and when to administer.
- In the final analysis, there is no single security formula that's right for everybody. Each person must ultimately adopt precautions that suit his or her particular circumstances, instincts, and personal preferences. Once you understand what your choices are, total coverage comes down to *what works best for you.*

That about does it. Again, we hope that *Total Coverage* fulfills its intended purpose of helping you to safeguard most effectively all the things you care about most—your family, your life, your health, and your property. May these pages prove useful in times of serious demand—but we hope even more that your call for total coverage instead grows out of the everyday need for a secure and protected life.

Appendix

Chapter 1: Health Insurance

Blue Cross/Blue Shield of America
676 North St. Clair Street
Chicago, IL 60611
Telephone: 312/440-6000
For local sources of Blue Cross/Blue Shield health insurance
see the Yellow Pages of your telephone directory.

The Health Insurance Fact and Answer Book
Geri Harrington, (Harper & Row, 1985)

The Medicare Answer Book
Geri Harrington, (Harper & Row, 1982)

The American Association of Retired Persons (AARP)
1909 K Street N.W.
Washington, DC 20049
For information on health insurance and older Americans.
Also for information on AARP'S own longterm custodial care policy.

The American Association of University Women
2401 Virginia Avenue, N.W.
Washington, DC 20037
Telephone: 202/785-7700

The National Organization of Women
425 13th Street, N.W.
Washington, DC 20004
Telephone: 202/347-2279

The Older Women's League (OWL)
1325 G Street N.W.
Washington, DC 20005
Telephone: 202/783-6686
For information on the League's group health insurance plans for
qualified women.

The Complete Guide to the New Tax Law
Gary L. Klott, (Times Books, 1986)

Chapter 2: Alternative Health Care Plans

The Group Health Association of America
1129 20th Street
Suite 600
Washington, DC 20036
Telephone: 202/778-3200
For general information on HMOs.

Chapter 3: Life Insurance

Insurance Information Institute
110 William Street
New York, NY 10038
Telephone: 800/221-4954 or 212/669-9200

National Insurance Consumer Organization
344 Commerce Street
Alexandria, VA 22314
Telephone: 703/549-8050

Best's Insurance Report
Check larger libraries for this source book, which rates
insurance companies as to financial stability.

American Council of Life Insurance
1850 K Street, N.W.
Washington, DC 20006
Telephone: 202/862-4000

The National Association of Insurance Commissioners (NAIC)
350 Bishops Way
Brookfield, WI 53005
Telephone: 414/784-9540

Chapter 4: Disability Income Insurance

Local Social Security offices. Look in the telephone directory under United States Government.

The National Insurance Consumer Organization
344 Commerce Street
Alexandria, VA 22314
Telephone: 703/549-8050

Chapter 5: Personal Safety

United States Pharmacopeial Convention, Inc. (USP)
12601 Twinbrook Parkway
Rockville, MD 20852
Telephone: 301/881-0666
For "Tips Against Tampering" contact USP (Attn. Dept. TC)

Consumer Product Safety Commission
1111 18th Street, N.W.
Washington, DC 20207
Telephone: 1-800/638-2772

Consumer Federation of America
1421 16th Street N.W.
Suite 604
Washington, DC 20036
Telephone: 202/387-6121

Major Appliance Consumer Action Panel (MACAP)
20 North Wacker Drive
Chicago, IL 60606
Re: product warranties and consumer complaint procedures.

The Product Safety Book
Brobeck/Averyt, (Dutton, 1983)

Mothers Against Drunk Driving (MADD)
    5330 Primrose
    Suite 146
    Fair Oaks, CA 95628
    Telephone: 916/966-6233

Crime Prevention Coalition (crime tips)
    P.O. Box 6700
    Rockville, MD 20850
    Re: crime tips and information on National Citizens' Crime
    Prevention Campaign

National Center for Missing and Exploited Children
    1835 K Street, N.W.
    Washington, DC 20006
    Telephone: 202/634-9821
    National Hotline: 1-800/843-5678

National Committee for Prevention of Child Abuse
    P.O. Box 2866
    Chicago, IL 60690
    Telephone: 312/565-1100

National Crime Prevention Institute
    School of Police Administration
    University of Louisville, Shelby Campus
    Louisville, KY 40222
    Telephone: 502/588-6987

Protect Your Child
    Laura Huchton, (Prentice-Hall, Inc., 1985)

The Family Guide to Crime Prevention
    Estrella/Forst, (Beaufort, 1981)

The Affordable Baby
    Darcie Bundy, (Harper & Row, 1985)

National Safety Council
    444 North Michigan Avenue
    Chicago, IL 60611
    Telephone: 312/727-4800

National Highway Traffic Safety Administration
    400 Seventh Street, S.W.
    Washington, DC 20590

Chapter 6: Homeowner's Insurance

American Institute of Real Estate Appraisers
430 North Michigan Avenue
Chicago, IL 60611
Telephone: 312/440-8141
Check Yellow Pages for a designated Member of the Appraiser's Institute (MAI) in your area.

The Insurance Information Institute
110 William Street
New York, NY 10038
Telephone: 212/669-9200 or 1-800/221-4954

The Federal Crime Insurance Program
P.O. Box 41033
Washington, DC 20014
Telephone: 1-800/638-8780

National Association of Public Insurance Adjusters
300 Water Street
Baltimore, MD 21202
Telephone: 301/539-4141

Federal Insurance Administration
(Flood Insurance Program)
Telephone: 1-800/683-6620

Chapter 7: Automobile Insurance and Car Security Systems

Insurance Information Institute
110 William Street
New York, NY 10038
Telephone: 212/669-9200 or 1-800/221-4954
For booklets "Insurance for the Car" and "Auto Insurance Basics"

National Insurance Consumer Organization
344 Commerce Street
Alexandria, VA 22314
For booklet "Buyer's Guide to Insurance"

Chapter 8: Basic Home Security

Insurance Information Institute
110 William Street
New York, NY 10038
Telephone: 212/669-9200 or 1-800/221-4954
For booklet "Home Security Basics"

Texas Crime Prevention Institute
Southwest Texas State University
San Marcos, TX 78666
For "Operation Identification" information in your area contact your local police.

New York Times, July 10, 1986
"Securing the Home to Keep Would-Be Burglars at Bay"

Chapter 9: Home Security Systems

National Burglar and Fire Alarm Association (NBFAA)
1120 19th Street, N.W.
Washington, DC 20036
Telephone: 202/296-9595

New York Times, July 10, 1986
"Alarm Systems That Are Easy to Install"

Chapter 10: Writing a Will

Contact a lawyer who specializes in estate law in your area.

Index